MIKHAIL BAKHTIN

Mikhail Bakhtin was one of the twentieth century's most influential literary theorists. This accessible introduction to his thought begins with the questions 'Why Bakhtin?' and 'Who was Bakhtin?', before dealing in detail with his ideas on authorship and subjecthood, language, dialogism, heteroglossia and the novel, the chronotope, and the carnivalesque. True to their dialogic spirit, these ideas are presented not as a fixed body of knowledge, but rather as living and evolving entities, as ways of approaching not only the most persistent questions of language and literature, but also issues that are relevant across the full range of Humanities disciplines. Bakhtin emerges in the process as a key thinker for the Humanities in the twenty-first century.

Alastair Renfrew is Reader in English and Comparative Literature at Durham University, UK.

ROUTLEDGE CRITICAL THINKERS

Series Editor: Robert Eaglestone, Royal Holloway, University of London

Routledge Critical Thinkers is a series of accessible introductions to key figures in contemporary critical thought.

With a unique focus on historical and intellectual contexts, the volumes in this series examine important theorists':

- significance
- motivation
- key ideas and sources
- impact on other thinkers

Concluding with extensively annotated guides to further reading, *Routledge Critical Thinkers* are the student's passport to today's most exciting critical thought.

Also available in the series:

MIKHAIL BAKHTIN

Alastair Renfrew

Routledge
Taylor & Francis Group

LONDON AND NEW YORK

First published 2015
by Routledge
2 Park Square, Milton Park, Abingdon, Oxon OX14 4RN

and by Routledge
711 Third Avenue, New York, NY 10017

*Routledge is an imprint of the Taylor & Francis Group, an
informa business*

British Library Cataloguing-in-Publication Data
A catalogue record for this book is available from the British
Library

Library of Congress Cataloging in Publication Data
Renfrew, Alistair.
Mikhail Bakhtin / Alastair Renfrew.
pages cm. -- (Routledge critical thinkers)
Includes bibliographical references and index.
1. Bakhtin, M. M. (Mikhail Mikhailovich), 1895-1975--
Criticism and interpretation. 2. Criticism--History--20th
century. 3. Literature--History and criticism--Theory, etc.
I. Title.
PN81.R373 2014
801'.95--dc23
2014026140

ISBN: 978-0-415-31968-3 (hbk)
ISBN: 978-0-415-31969-0 (pbk)
ISBN: 978-0-203-62550-7 (ebk)

Typeset in Sabon
by Taylor & Francis Books

CONTENTS

SERIES EDITOR'S PREFACE

The books in this series offer introductions to major critical thinkers who have influenced literary studies and the humanities. The *Routledge Critical Thinkers* series provides the books you can turn to first when a new name or concept appears in your studies.

Each book will equip you to approach a key thinker's original texts by explaining his or her key ideas, putting them into context and, perhaps most importantly, showing you why this thinker is considered to be significant. The emphasis is on concise, clearly written guides which do not presuppose a specialist knowledge. Although its focus is on particular figures, the series stresses that critical thinkers never existed in a vacuum, but instead emerged from broader intellectual, cultural and social contexts. Finally, these books will act as a bridge between you and the thinkers' original texts: not replacing them, but rather complementing what they wrote. In some cases, volumes consider small clusters of thinkers working in the same area, developing similar ideas or influencing each other.

These books are necessary for a number of reasons. In his 1997 autobiography, *Not Entitled*, the literary critic Frank Kermode wrote of a time in the 1960s:

> On beautiful summer lawns, young people lay together all night, recovering from their daytime exertions and listening to a troupe of Balinese

> musicians. Under their blankets or their sleeping bags, they would chat
> drowsily about the gurus of the time ... What they repeated was largely
> hearsay; hence my lunchtime suggestion, quite impromptu, for a series of
> short, very cheap books offering authoritative but intelligible introductions
> to such figures.

There is still a need for 'authoritative and intelligible introductions'.
But this series reflects a different world from the 1960s. New thinkers have emerged, and the reputations of others have risen and
fallen as new research has developed. New methodologies and
challenging ideas have spread through the arts and humanities. The
study of literature is no longer – if it ever was – simply the study
and evaluation of poems, novels and plays. It is also the study of
ideas, issues and difficulties which arise in any literary text and in
its interpretation. Other arts and humanities subjects have changed
in analogous ways.

With these changes, new problems have emerged. The ideas and
issues behind these radical changes in the humanities are often
presented without reference to wider contexts or as theories which
you can simply 'add on' to the texts you read. Certainly, there's
nothing wrong with picking out selected ideas or using what comes
to hand – indeed, some thinkers have argued that this is, in fact, all
we can do. However, it is sometimes forgotten that each new idea
comes from the pattern and development of somebody's thought
and that it is important to study the range and context of their
ideas. Against theories 'floating in space', the *Routledge Critical
Thinkers* series places key thinkers and their ideas firmly back in
their contexts.

More than this, these books reflect the need to go back to the
thinkers' own texts and ideas. Every interpretation of an idea, even
the most seemingly innocent one, offers you its own 'spin', implicitly or explicitly. To read only books on a thinker, rather than
texts by that thinker, is to deny yourself a chance of making up
your own mind. Sometimes what makes a significant figure's work
hard to approach is not so much its style or its content as the
feeling of not knowing where to start. The purpose of these books
is to give you a 'way in' by offering an accessible overview of these
thinkers' ideas and works and by guiding your further reading,
starting with each thinker's own texts. To use a metaphor from the

philosopher Ludwig Wittgenstein (1889–1951), these books are
ladders that are to be thrown away after you have climbed to the
next level. Not only, then, do they equip you to approach new
ideas, but they also empower you by leading you back to the theorist's own texts and encouraging you to develop your own
informed opinions.

Finally, these books are necessary because, just as intellectual
needs have changed radically, so too have the education systems
around the world – the contexts in which introductory books are
usually read. What was suitable for the minority higher education
systems of the 1960s is not suitable for the larger, wider, more
diverse, high technology education systems of the twenty-first century. These changes call not just for new, up-to-date introductions,
but new methods of presentation as well. The presentational
aspects of the *Routledge Critical Thinkers* series have been developed
with today's students in mind.

Each book in the series has a similar structure. They begin with
a section offering an overview of the life and ideas of the featured
thinker and explain why they are important. The central section of
each book discusses the thinker's key ideas, his or her context,
evolution and reception; with the books that deal with more than
one thinker, they also explain and explore the influence of each on
each. The volumes conclude with a survey of the impact of the
thinker or thinkers, outlining how their ideas have been taken up
and developed by others. In addition, there is a detailed final section suggesting and describing books for further reading. This is
not a 'tacked-on' section, but an integral part of each volume. In
the first part of this section, you will find brief descriptions of the
thinker's key works, then, following this, information on the most
useful critical works and, in some cases, on relevant websites. This
section will guide you in your reading, enabling you to follow your
interests and develop your own projects. Throughout each book,
references are given in what is known as the Harvard system (the
author and the date of a work cited are given in the text and you
can look up the full details in the bibliography at the back). This
offers a lot of information in very little space. The books also
explain technical terms and use boxes to describe events or ideas in
more detail – away from the main emphasis of the discussion.
Boxes are also used at times to highlight definitions of terms

frequently used or coined by a thinker. In this way, the boxes serve as a kind of glossary, since they are easily identified when flicking through the book.

The thinkers in the series are 'critical' for three reasons. First, they are examined in the light of subjects which involve criticism: principally literary studies or English and cultural studies, but also other disciplines which rely on the criticism of books, ideas, theories and unquestioned assumptions. Second, they are critical because studying their work will provide you with a 'tool kit' for your own informed critical reading and thought, which will make you critical. Third, these thinkers are critical because they are crucially important: they deal with ideas and questions which can overturn conventional understandings of the world, of texts, of everything we take for granted, leaving us with a deeper understanding of what we already knew and with new ideas.

No introduction can tell you everything. However, by offering a way into critical thinking, this series hopes to begin to engage you in an activity which is productive, constructive and potentially life-changing.

ACKNOWLEDGEMENTS

This book, like all books, is a product of dialogue. I'd therefore like to acknowledge and thank everyone who has written on Bakhtin, from the briefest word to the most comprehensive study, from those who have provoked instant recognition to those who have produced violent disagreement; all have contributed to the 'conversation', which, despite occasional indicators to the contrary, is far from being over. There are also a large number of colleagues and friends who have little interest in Bakhtin, but who have, in many and various ways, helped write this book. The smaller number of people who have actively got in the way of its writing have my sympathies.

Special thanks go to John, big Moira, wee Moira, Anna, Ellie, Alex and Kim. Finally, warm thanks go to the series editor Robert Eaglestone, who has helped spare readers a great deal of unnecessary pain, and to Polly Dodson, Ruth Hilsdon and Liz Levine at Routledge, all of whom have proven that patience is a virtue – and virtue is always its own reward.

ABBREVIATIONS

AH   'Author and Hero in Aesthetic Activity', in *Art and Answerability*, pp. 5–256.

BSHR   'The *Bildungsroman* and its Significance in the History of Realism (Toward a Historical Typology of the Novel)', in *Speech Genres and Other Late Essays*, pp. 10–59.

DLDP   'Discourse in Life and Discourse in Poetry', *Bakhtin School Papers*, ed. Ann Shukman (trans. John Richmond) (Russian Poetics in Translation, vol. 10) (Oxford: RTP Publications, 1983), pp. 5–30.

DN   'Discourse in the Novel', in *The Dialogic Imagination*, pp. 259–422.

EN   'Epic and Novel', in *The Dialogic Imagination*, pp. 3–41.

F   Voloshinov, *Freudianism*.

FM   Medvedev/Bakhtin, *The Formal Method in Literary Scholarship: A Critical Introduction to Sociological Poetics*.

FTC   'Forms of Time and of the Chronotope in the Novel: Notes toward a Historical Poetics', in *The Dialogic Imagination,* pp. 84–258.

MPL	Voloshinov, *Marxism and the Philosophy of Language*.
N70	'Notes Made in 1970–71', in *Speech Genres and Other Late Essays*, pp. 132–58.
PCMF	'The Problem of Content, Material and Form in Verbal Art', in *Art and Answerability*, pp. 257–325.
PDP	*Problems of Dostoevsky's Poetics*.
PND	'From the Prehistory of Novelistic Discourse', in *The Dialogic Imagination*, pp. 41–83.
PSG	'The Problem of Speech Genres', in *Speech Genres and Other Late Essays*, pp. 60–102.
PT	'The Problem of the Text in Linguistics, Philology, and the Human Sciences: An Experiment in Philosophical Analysis', in *Speech Genres and Other Late Essays*, pp. 103–31.
RQ	'Response to a Question from the Editorial Staff of *Novyi mir*', in *Speech Genres and Other Late Essays*, pp. 1–9.
RW	*Rabelais and His World*.
TMHS	'Toward a Methodology for the Human Sciences', in *Speech Genres and Other Late Essays*, pp. 159–77.
TPA	*Toward a Philosophy of the Act*.

WHY BAKHTIN?

Mikhail Mikhaiovich Bakhtin (1895–1975) was without doubt the most astonishingly productive thinker in the Humanities to emerge from Soviet Russia and one of the twentieth century's most significant theoreticians of literature. This book will show that Bakhtin's ideas remain crucial for literary studies, but also that his approach to literature remains, indeed, astonishingly productive across the full range of the contemporary Humanities. Bakhtin is a thinker who not only reconceives the relationship between literature and other disciplines, but who is also ultimately able to demonstrate the vital and common basis of all Humanities disciplines – of all disciplines that have *writing* at their conceptual and methodological core. As both the Soviet context and the twentieth century itself recede into history, he has become one of the most important thinkers for the Humanities in the twenty-first century.

Bakhtin is, in fact, an *exemplary* thinker for the contemporary Humanities, for a number of reasons: because his broad philosophical grounding and profoundly ethical focus does not conflict with, but rather enhances, his literary conception; because his investment in ideas of collectivity does not contradict his enduring commitment to the individual consciousness; and because his best-known ideas – the dialogic, heteroglossia, chronotope, carnival – emerge from a lifelong engagement with the novel form, but find renewed force and justification beyond the purely literary domain.

The roots of Bakhtin's attraction lie to some extent in the fact that, although he became known in the West during a period of huge growth of interest in literary and cultural theory in the 1970s, 1980s and 1990s, his thought does not share the central tendency of the key theoretical paradigms such as Structuralism, Marxism, Psychoanalysis and Deconstruction. These paradigms, for all the many and profound ways in which they diverge from and even contradict one another, are nonetheless related by a common characteristic: they are all broadly *hermeneuticist*, that is, they all imply the existence of *another* 'text' beneath the surface or in the interstices of the text or discourse under interpretation. The meaning of any utterance has increasingly been held to lie somewhere beneath or beyond the surface intention of its speaker or author – to the point where the very presence of an author of a literary work or a 'subject' of discourse comes into question. For Bakhtin, however, the presence and self-constitution of the speaking subject (sometimes, indeed, an author) lies at the heart of any process of human understanding; it is the inalienable core of his thought. He offers, therefore, a way of understanding the complex relationship between text and world on the basis of the *presence* of the human subject (or subjects) without colluding in crude, one-dimensional theories of intentionality. Bakhtin never departs from a core Humanistic position, but instead theorizes (re-theorizes) the conditions of possibility of Humanism 'after theory' by theorizing the various modes of being and expression – literary and non-literary – of the living, speaking subject. Meaning for Bakhtin is irreducibly present in, but not simplistically reducible to, the text; it is what philosophers would call 'immanent'. This, in the end, is what texts (and speech) are for.

IMMANENCE

Borrowed from Theology by way of Philosophy, *immanence* describes the way in which the properties of a given concept or phenomenon – such as, foundationally, God – are said to inhere in the concept or phenomenon itself. In literary studies, the idea of immanence opens up questions about the limits of the text: are texts self-contained, autonomous and complete on their own terms? Does the meaning of the text appear in the words on the page, does it need to be read in its social and historical context, or in the context of the author's life? And are these positions mutually exclusive? One of the basic constants of Bakhtin's work is a desire to break down the apparent opposition between theories of the immanence of the literary text (formalist approaches) and theories of its determination by the external environment (contextual, sociological, historical approaches); or, to use a term that will recur in his work, to concentrate on what happens on the *boundaries* between such theories. Bakhtin's core ideas on the dialogic nature of speech and writing suggest that meaning is in one sense immanent in the utterance or the literary work, while it is at the same time intensely connected to the environment in which it is produced. His thought ultimately seeks to erase any comfortable distinction between what is intrinsic and what is extrinsic to the literary work or, indeed, to any utterance.

Another aspect of Bakhtin's attraction is that he consistently approaches questions of the construction of the human subject, of meaning and of ethics not through the formal lens of philosophy or linguistics, but through the endlessly diffuse lens of literature. His thought returns again and again to the question of what is at stake in the connection between literature and the world beyond it, but it always maintains the primacy of the *text*, which is never reduced in Bakhtin's hands to the status of a mere reflection of something else. The 'kind' of literature Bakhtin is primarily interested in is the novel, or at least the ways in which novels (or some novels) manifest his idea of 'novelness', which becomes at different points a near synonym for his key category of the dialogic. Reading Bakhtin can therefore provide, at the most basic of levels, a range of uniquely powerful insights into the novel, but it can also, as we have suggested, help us expand upon those insights in ways that exceed the scope of the novel or even literature itself, contextualizing it against what Bakhtin will call the 'universal' of the dialogic. The nature of boundaries 'between' literature and the world, or more properly, the way these and other phenomena merge across or entirely deconstruct boundaries, is what makes reading Bakhtin a task that generates often unexpected rewards.

The phenomenon that dramatizes and binds together the various elements of Bakhtin's work, more so even than literature, is language. Whether in the context of everyday life, in the mouths of real people or on the pages of literary works, in the mouths of Bakhtin's no less real 'authors and heroes', language both embodies and provides access to the various phases of human experience. Bakhtin and his colleagues, in pursuit of a deeper understanding of the fullness of such experience, will offer their own theory of language, built around the 'utterance' as the emblem of a 'living language', as opposed to the rules and conventions of language as an abstract system. Language may be the stuff of life as it is lived and at the same time the self-evident point of embarkation for literary study, but it is also the common denominator of the Humanities – it is the high road of interdisciplinarity. Bakhtin's invocation in the related fields of sociolinguistics, anthropology, social theory, and of course philosophy, from which he initially comes, is a testament to the fact that what is important for and in Bakhtin – the construction and transmission of meaning and the relation of the self to the other – is central to the Humanities project at large. The best-known works of Bakhtin's middle period, such as his book on Dostoevsky and 'Discourse in the Novel', are all in some ways dependent on the elaboration of a theory of language – a 'translinguistics' as we will call it in Chapter 5. His later and sometimes fragmentary 'essays' of the 1960s and 1970s make more explicit the relationship between that theory of language and a central, binding idea of the Humanities. The questions raised there – regarding the status of the text, the relationship of lived experience to its literary or theoretical inscription – are the questions that resound through the broad mainstream of the contemporary Humanities, manifest in each of its component disciplines in different ways – but in ways that can be routed and related through Bakhtin.

This book will begin, however, by returning to Bakhtin's earliest work, written but unpublished in the 1920s, in order to explore the model of self-other relations developed there, which underpins his later ideas on the significance of language and the more familiar categories of dialogism, heteroglossia, chronotope and carnival. It will then deal with what might be regarded as a key turning point in Bakhtin's life and work, the alignment of his work with the work of his friends and colleagues Valentin Voloshinov and Pavel Medvedev, and, especially, the significance of the former in relation to what has come to be known as the 'linguistic turn' in philosophy and the Humanities more broadly. On this dual basis, we will then devote separate chapters to dialogism, heteroglossia, chronotope and carnival, in each case tracing the ways in which these ideas evolve in a process of mutual definition with the 'core' of Bakhtin's initial conception. This trajectory will be completed by a chapter on genre, which brings together strands from every phase of Bakhtin's work and reconnects to some of the questions we have already encountered, questions of the 'boundaries' between literature and life. The book will then conclude with a brief assessment not so much of Bakhtin's influence, but of his continuing *usefulness*, both to readers interested primarily in literature and in the context of the Humanities in general.

The book can be read in three ways: first, some readers may wish simply to read continuously from the first chapter to the last, encountering Bakhtin's major concepts in the context of his thought as a whole and in the process of its evolution; other readers might wish to begin with the chapter on dialogism, move through the mature concepts of heteroglossia, chronotope and carnival, and then return to the earlier chapters in order to explore the roots from which they emerged; finally, the chapters can be read separately as individual treatments of specific concepts, the reader accepting or rejecting invitations to connect with other areas of Bakhtin's thought according to his or her own inclination.

Bakhtin prefaced one of his own early works, 'The Problem of Content, Material and Form in Verbal Art', with a declaration of its freedom 'from the superfluous ballast of citation and reference, [...] unnecessary for the competent reader, and of no help whatever to the incompetent reader' (PCMF 257). While it is not possible in the present context to duplicate Bakhtin's rather cavalier attitude, citation and reference is focused heavily on Bakhtin's own writings (and relevant literary exemplars) and has been kept to a minimum in relation to other critical and theoretical sources. Citation is from the editions referred to in the 'Abbreviations' section at the beginning of the book, full details of which are given under 'Further reading' at the end; translations have been modified slightly in certain cases.

Throughout the book, as is hopefully already abundantly clear, we will return again and again to the fundamentally literary significance of Bakhtin's work, the sense in which his ideas cannot live in separation from literary categories, and at the same time to its similarly marked portability, the sense in which his ideas demand to be understood – and exercise profound effects – in contexts that are not conventionally regarded as 'literary'. If this book has a core hypothesis of its own, it is that the Bakhtin who provides powerful resources for the study of literature is entirely consistent with the Bakhtin who stands at the heart of a differently conceived Humanities. In both the content and the practice of his thought, Bakhtin casts the boundaries between disciplines in an entirely different light – a light that only becomes fully visible after Bakhtin.

First, however, consistent with Bakhtin's insistence on the presence and significance of the living, speaking subject, with his fearlessness in the face of 'biographical' reductiveness, we will consider the no less essential question of 'who' Bakhtin was.

2

WHO WAS BAKHTIN?

Bakhtin lived the majority of his life in almost complete obscurity, before enjoying a belated and unexpected period of academic fame in the Soviet Union in the 1960s and early 1970s. He published only one significant book, on the great Russian novelist of the nineteenth century, Fedor Dostoevsky (1821–81), close to the time at which it was written; most of his work saw the light of day only after his death, with the major exception of another book, on the Renaissance author François Rabelais (c. 1494–1553), which was published in 1965, almost thirty years after it was begun. At the time of his death in 1975, Bakhtin was known outside the Soviet Union (and outside a small circle of Western Slavists) only as the author of the book on Rabelais, the central idea of which – carnival – had found a welcoming audience on publication in English translation in 1968. The details of his biography and career, particularly certain aspects of his earlier life and his time in exile in the 1930s, have acquired a sense of mystery, which only intensified as his name became recognized in the West. His name and his significance have been consistently surrounded by a certain almost mythical aura, which, although it helped propel him towards an extensive readership, particularly in the 1980s and 1990s, has tended to obscure the nature and value of his thought. This makes it all the more important, before addressing the question of why

Bakhtin's thought remains of use to us and elucidating his key ideas, to deal first with how 'Bakhtin' has been mediated and to examine with more than the usual degree of caution the ways in which the canon of his work and the changing perceptions of his persona have been constructed.

There are many good reasons why Bakhtin's work and personality have been shrouded in doubt, and even mystery: the cultural and political circumstances of the late 1910s and 1920s in Russia and the Soviet Union, which problematized and in many cases destroyed the public lives of countless scholars, critics and writers; the Stalinist era that followed, in which individuals or cultural tendencies that would not or could not make a bargain with State ideology were excluded or annihilated, forcing Russian intellectual culture into a kind of ice age; the consequently fractured process of the publication of Bakhtin's work in Russia, where no major critical or theoretical work appeared in his name between 1929 and 1963; the fact that a number of texts published under the names of Bakhtin's friends and colleagues, Valentin Voloshinov (1895–1936) and Pavel Medvedev (1892–1938), were subsequently claimed to be the work of Bakhtin himself; and, finally, the rather fractured process of the translation of his work into English, which was rendered all the more problematic in that it has been accompanied by the intermittent appearance of 'new' material in Russia.

There are also a number of less obvious – but nevertheless indisputably significant – reasons why Bakhtin has acquired this sense of mystery. Consistent with one of the enduring stereotypes of Soviet Russia, he was sent into exile in 1930 – not, as the initial sentence decreed, to a labour camp, where the fragile Bakhtin would almost certainly have perished, but to a job as a bookkeeper in Kustanai in distant Kazakhstan. The sentence was commuted because of Bakhtin's poor state of health and because of the interventions of two extremely influential cultural figures: Bakhtin's book on Dostoevsky had been reviewed favourably by the former People's Commissar for Enlightenment, Anatolii Lunacharskii (1875–1933), and the most politically influential writer of the period, Maxim Gorky (1868–1936), intervened personally on Bakhtin's behalf. Bakhtin's health would in fact play a doubly significant role in his mythologization: the osteomyelitis that effectively saved his life in 1930 would later result in the amputation of his left leg at the knee, leaving the amputee scholar with the most dramatic bodily symbol of his victimhood – and of his survivorhood.

Bakhtin himself was not averse to myth-making. He is a consistently unreliable source for his own biography and appears, for example, to have borrowed parts of his brother Nikolai's biography in order to bolster an extremely thin – and possibly non-existent – formal higher education: Bakhtin may never have attended university, as he claimed, and he certainly never graduated. He was more tentative, much later in life, regarding the supposition that he had come from an aristocratic background, a caution not shared by the émigré Nikolai, who was keen to emphasize their father's status as a fallen noble as opposed to the bourgeois banker he in fact was. Neither version of the Bakhtins' background was particularly promising at the most class-conscious points in Soviet history, but the mythological slippage is typical.

Bakhtin is also a contradictory witness in the matter of the authorship of Voloshinov's *Freudianism* (1927) and *Marxism and the Philosophy of Language* (1929) and Medvedev's *The Formal Method in Literary Studies* (1928), sometimes implying his own participation, at the very least, and at other times steadfastly defending the authorship of his friends. He often displays the casual disregard for academic convention befitting someone who lived an entire life outside, or on the periphery of, the academic system: sections of *Rabelais and His World*, for example, appear to have been lifted wholesale from the German philosopher Ernst Cassirer (1874–1945). And the anecdotal evidence of contemporaries – often repeating Bakhtin's own self-characterization – consistently emphasizes his unorthodoxy, mysticism, or even fatalism. This is never more dramatic than in the alleged fate of his book on the novel of education or *Bildungsroman*: the typescript may indeed have perished in the publisher's offices under German bombing, but did the chain-smoking Bakhtin, starved of cigarette papers during the Nazi invasion, really roll the only surviving copy up and smoke it?

The key factor in catalysing all of these circumstances into a thoroughgoing myth pertains as much to Bakhtin's 'second life' of rediscovery and transmission into the West as it does to his first of relative obscurity in the Soviet Union. The fragmented process of Bakhtin's reception in the West was accompanied by – or perhaps, more accurately, *caused* – the rise of what has been described as the Bakhtin 'industry', which experienced its very own 'boom' in the late 1980s and early 1990s. Sceptics have expressed surprise that, while other theorists – with the certain exception of the French-Algerian philosopher and founder of deconstruction Jacques Derrida (1930–2004) and the French philosopher and cultural historian Michel Foucault (1926–84), and possibly also such thinkers as the German literary and cultural theorist Walter Benjamin (1892–1940) – have had relatively little exposure outside the confines of their own discipline, an entire 'industry' should grow up around the figure of Bakhtin. We will examine the substantive elements in Bakhtin's work that contributed to this surge in his popularity in due course, but for the moment it is important to focus on the key circumstantial reason, which is once again relatively simple. Bakhtin, precisely *because* of the interruptions and chronological disordering of his publication and translation, emerged in the West with a kind of 'delayed effect' right at the point when the various strands that had propelled literary theory in France and the English-speaking world – chiefly, Marxism, Structuralism and Deconstruction – were beginning to be perceived in terms of their limitations, rather than their productive potential. Before turning to his 'second' life in the West, however, we must first examine in greater detail the story of Bakhtin's 'real' life in Russia and the Soviet Union.

PETROGRAD, NEVEL AND VITEBSK

The same Bakhtin who would go on to champion the 'low' genres of everyday speech and the democratizing power of the novel and who, at least in one of his Western incarnations, would be associated with a broadly Marxist conception of literature and culture welcomed the triumph of Bolshevism in Russia in suitably contradictory style. A few weeks short of his twenty-second birthday, and apparently contemptuous of the dirty political realities of the street, Bakhtin claims to have spent the days between the February and October Revolutions of 1917 cocooned in a Petrograd reading room, at least 'when the heating was turned on'. This is entirely consistent with the young Bakhtin's experience in the revolutionary years in terms both of his attitude to practical politics and its intimation of the recurrent theme of material hardship.

THE REVOLUTIONS OF 1917

The abdication of Tsar Nikolai II in February 1917, which took place at the peak of events that have been labelled the 'February Revolution' and which occurred against the backdrop of the ongoing First World War, propelled the Russian Empire into a period of often chaotic political unrest. A series of provisional governments not only failed to establish political and economic stability, but also reconfirmed Russia's commitment to the war, before a failed military coup in August precipitated perhaps the most astonishing and far-reaching event in modern European history. The Marxist and anti-war Bolshevik Party, led by Vladimir Ilyich Lenin (1870–1924), despite the lack of any significant political base outside the major cities, managed to manoeuvre its way towards a bravura seizure of power in what is termed the 'October Revolution' (although it actually took place in November according to the Western calendar). The Revolution in turn precipitated a period of revolutionary or civil war, which brought with it incredible hardship. The political and economic situation began to normalize after the Bolshevik victory in the civil war, with the initiation of Lenin's 'New Economic Policy' in 1921 and the preparations for a new state, The Union of Soviet Socialist Republics (USSR), which was inaugurated in December 1922. The early to mid-1920s, although marked by the entrenchment of one-party rule, was also a period of relative cultural pluralism, which produced significant achievements in literature, cinema, painting and the plastic arts, and, perhaps not least, in the development of literary theory.

Partly because there was food there, in contrast to a starving Petrograd, and partly also because he had no particular wish to be anywhere near the heart of political upheaval, Bakhtin moved in 1918 to Nevel (in modern Belarus), where he took a post as a secondary teacher. Bakhtin's path to Nevel was probably cleared by Lev Pumpianskii (1891–1940), one of the early Soviet period's most talented literary critics whose reputation has yet to be fully reconstructed; Bakhtin and Pumpianskii would be joined in Nevel by Matvei Kagan (1889–1937), who had studied philosophy in Marburg and Berlin under Hermann Cohen (1842–1918) and Paul

Natorp (1854–1924), followers and re-interpreters of Immanuel Kant (1724–1804) who are therefore often referred to as 'neo-Kantians'. Bakhtin, Pumpianskii and Kagan participated for a time in a seminar on Kant, which formed the initial core of a 'Bakhtin Circle', although the term would later be associated more with Voloshinov and Medvedev. While neo-Kantian ethics underpin Bakhtin's first published work, the extremely short essay 'Art and Answerability' (1919), it was the other significant strand in his early thought, Christianity, that made his relationship with the Bolshevik authorities who were transforming Russian society, including the education system in which Bakhtin worked, less than comfortable.

Bakhtin moved in 1920 to Vitebsk to take up a post as lecturer in European literature. Here, he was surrounded by a quite different cultural environment, which included the Modernist painters Marc Chagall (1887–1985) and Kazimir Malevich (1879–1935), as well as Pumpianskii, Voloshinov – whom Bakhtin had met in Nevel – and a new face, Pavel Medvedev; the 'Circle', inasmuch as the description is accurate, was all but complete. Despite his continuing struggle with illness and with the seemingly intractable problem of securing a permanent academic post, Bakhtin begins to emerge in the Vitebsk years as a thinker of considerable stature: he continued work on what would later become *Toward a Philosophy of the Act*, begun in Nevel; more importantly, he begins the process of transition from consideration of purely ethical questions to engagement with aesthetics (although ethics, in one form or another, would remain central to his work throughout his life). The first significant product of this transition has survived only in incomplete form as 'Author and Hero in Aesthetic Activity', the earliest comprehensive statement of Bakhtin's model of self-other relations; it is almost certainly the case, however, that Bakhtin was also at this time writing the first draft of his book on Dostoevsky, which would be published in extensively revised form only in 1929, when his thought – and his circumstances – had undergone significant change.

LENINGRAD AND THE DISPUTED TEXTS

In 1924, Bakhtin returned to the city (now renamed Leningrad after the death of Lenin in January of that year) he had been forced to leave six years earlier. Bakhtin lived a strange and difficult life in the new Leningrad, never managing to make an even half-way secure living from academic work. The resultant hand-to-mouth existence, based on occasional lecturing, tutoring, writing and editing, was one of the factors – we can only speculate on the others – that may have involved him in a series of convoluted publishing transactions with friends and colleagues in the 'Circle', including Voloshinov and Medvedev.

The first work Bakhtin attempted to publish in his own name during this period is further evidence of his steady movement from ethics to aesthetics. A blend of precise analysis and withering polemic against the Formalism which had quickly come to dominate Russian literary criticism, 'The Problem of Content, Material and Form in Verbal Art', unlike so many of Bakhtin's 'lost' or 'recovered' texts, was commissioned by one of the few journals then functioning without the intervention of censorship, *Russkii sovremennik* [*The Russian Contemporary*], which was edited by the same Maxim Gorky who would later intervene on Bakhtin's behalf and help secure his release from exile. The journal was closed before Bakhtin's essay could be published.

Here, one strand of the mystery begins: shortly after the closure of *Russkii sovremennik*, Medvedev, who appears to have been considerably more 'worldly' and practical than Bakhtin, published an in some ways similar critique of Formalism, 'Academic Salierism: On the Formal (Morphological) Method', in the journal *Zvezda* [*The Star*], and the question of the 'disputed texts' was born. Medvedev would go on to publish another article in *Zvezda* in the following year on the subject of the sociological approach to literature and, in 1928, the book *The Formal Method in Literary Studies*, which the balance of Russian commentators still hold to be substantially the work of Bakhtin.

It is less easy to see the connection between Bakhtin's institutional exclusion and resultant publishing difficulties and two strands of work published under the name of Voloshinov. The first was a bold critique of the founder of psychoanalysis, Sigmund Freud (1856–1939), contained in a 1926 article for *Zvezda* and the book *Freudianism* (1927). The second was built around a critique of the Saussurean linguistics that would nevertheless go on to become a significant force in the rise of literary theory, particularly in the West. Voloshinov's response to Saussure is contained in a series of articles and the precociously brilliant book *Marxism and the Philosophy of Language* (1929), the title of which, it ought to be said, is belied by much of its content. Again, these works have often been attributed to Bakhtin, despite the fact that no secure documentary proof has emerged in the eighty years since their publication; evidence in support of Bakhtin's authorship is in fact consistently anecdotal and has been memorably dismissed as 'reminiscences about reminiscences'.

It is worth acknowledging, however, that those who support Bakhtin's authorship of the major works published under the names of Voloshinov and Medvedev have been encouraged in that conviction, albeit indirectly, by a confirmed precedent: another friend, Ivan Kanaev (1893–1984), has admitted (following the death of Bakhtin and all the members of the 'Circle') that Bakhtin did in fact write the article 'Contemporary Vitalism' published under Kanaev's name in 1926 and that he had simply borrowed the necessary literature from the library on Bakhtin's behalf. Whatever the truth about the disputed texts, there is considerable irony in the fact that in the single case where Bakhtin's authorship has been established beyond doubt, the subject is neither ethics nor aesthetics, neither Freud nor Saussure – it is biology (admittedly in relation to its philosophical context).

DOSTOEVSKY, ARREST AND EXILE

1928 and 1929 were fatal years in the history of Soviet society, marking as they did the end of the power struggle that propelled Joseph Stalin (1878–1953) to a position of unchallenged authority and presaging the onset of authoritarianism. These years would almost prove fatal also for Bakhtin. Even in the context of a life as varied as Bakhtin's, 1929, the year in which he would finally see a major work in print under his own name – *Problems of Dostoevsky's Art* – turned out to be the most dramatic of all. Although Bakhtin had almost certainly completed a draft of the book before or shortly after leaving Vitebsk, the published version is transformed: the first part of the book through the prism of Voloshinov's literary-linguistic works of the late 1920s – whether Bakhtin wrote them or merely played a 'dialogic' role in their composition – and the second part, to an even greater extent, through Bakhtin's encounter with the Formalists, who had a greater influence on Bakhtin than has been acknowledged. In *Problems of Dostoevsky's Art*, everything that Bakhtin has been thinking and writing about over a ten-year period begins to crystallize into a theory that justifies the name of 'dialogism'. This 'turn to language', enforced or otherwise, would not only persist in his work through the long years of obscurity that were to follow, it would also be a key element of his appeal in the West many decades later.

Before this first major completed work saw the light of day, a development that might in other circumstances have helped set him upon a new trajectory closer to the academic establishment, Bakhtin's life took an entirely different course. In the early hours of 24 December 1928, he was arrested on suspicion of involvement with the religious group *Resurrection*, later described by the authorities as an 'underground counter-revolutionary organization of the Right intelligentsia', whose ultimate aim was 'the overthrow of Soviet power'. As he lay in hospital recovering from an operation on his leg due to his worsening osteomyelitis, Bakhtin was sentenced to five years in exile, most probably in the Solovetskii camp in the far north; for someone in Bakhtin's condition, this was effectively a death sentence. Pleas from his wife, Elena, from Bakhtin himself, as well as from Gorky and the similarly high-profile writer Aleksei Tolstoy (1883–1945), persuaded the authorities to conduct a medical examination, the outcome of which not only confirmed his chronic osteomyelitis, but revealed that he had in the past suffered both tuberculosis and meningitis. In one of the seemingly inexplicable paradoxes that are so typical of the Soviet 1920s, the Dostoevsky book remained freely available for sale – and was reviewed by so high-profile a figure as Lunacharskii – even as its author remained under house arrest. As mentioned above, the sentence was eventually commuted to exile to Kazakhstan, where Bakhtin could be accompanied by Elena and retain access to medical assistance. Like his hero Dostoevsky, who had in his youth been subjected to preparations for a mock execution on dubious political charges, Bakhtin had been granted a reprieve.

THE STALIN ERA

Joseph Stalin emerged from the power struggle that followed the death of Lenin and embarked on a process of radical centralization of government and economy, which, along with the gradual retreat into itself implied by the renunciation of 'World Revolution' in favour of 'Socialism in One Country', would define the Soviet state for the majority of its existence. The process of centralization and extension of state influence into virtually every area of public life began in 1927–28 with the forced collectivization of agriculture and the radical centralization of industry into Five-Year Plans. This 'industrial revolution' necessitated a parallel reorganization of cultural and social life that has been referred to as a 'cultural revolution', which legitimated state control of all areas of Soviet cultural life – including publishing, broadcasting, education, and literature and the arts – bringing the relative cultural pluralism of the mid-1920s to an abrupt halt. The imperatives of state control of cultural and social life, as well as the preservation of Stalin's own authority, led eventually to a series of purges, which reached their almost unimaginable peak between 1936 and 1938, when, under the direction of Nikolai Ezhov (1895–1940), at least 700,000 Soviet citizens were executed (many more were imprisoned or exiled, a proportion of whom died in captivity in later years). Despite the interlude of the Second World War – referred to in Russia as 'The Great Patriotic War' – in which as many as 27 million Soviet citizens perished resisting Hitler, Stalin's autocratic authority was re-established in the postwar period and Soviet intellectual culture remained in a virtual 'deep freeze' until shortly before his death in 1953. A distinct, if limited, period of cultural and intellectual liberalization followed under Nikita Khrushchev (1894–1971), who rose to power on the back of the denunciation of the cult of Stalin's personality and whose period of rule is broadly referred to as the 'Thaw'.

This 'second chance' would soon begin to appear like something of a charm. Bakhtin may have been unlucky to find himself in the rural provinces just as Stalin's forced and accelerated collectivization of agriculture brought famine to millions, but his status as a political exile gave him access to the same food supply as local

Communist Party officials. More significantly, Kazakhstan would turn out to be a far safer location to sit out at least the early stages of the creeping rise of Stalin's repression against an ever-widening circle of the intellectual and professional classes. And, astonishingly, what may be Bakhtin's most significant work, 'Discourse in the Novel', was written, with little conscious thought of the possibility of publication, while he worked by day in the offices of the regional food-supply cooperative. 'Discourse in the Novel' not only develops much of the argument of the Dostoevsky book, it does so on the broad ground of the rise of the European novel, which is invested with properties and potentialities previously reserved for the 'exceptional' – or exemplary – case of Dostoevsky; it is not only Bakhtin's most enduringly productive work for literary studies, yielding the concepts of heteroglossia and hybridization (to which we will turn in Chapter 7), it is also his most accessible statement of the underlying concept of dialogism. Whatever the state of Bakhtin's mind during this seemingly hopeless period, he did pass a version of the typescript to Kagan in 1936, perhaps with the hope of its finding a publisher; it eventually did, but only in 1975, the year of his death.

ANOTHER FORM OF EXILE

Bakhtin's pursuit of an academic position brought him at the end of his exile not to Leningrad or to Moscow and its environs, but to the provincial city of Saransk, 350 miles to the east. In the autumn of 1936, partly through the assistance of Medvedev, he was appointed lecturer in world literature at the Mordovian Pedagogical Institute. Yet even a provincial teacher-training college was too close for comfort, institutionally if not geographically. Bakhtin had barely completed a term in his new post when, early in 1937, the year Stalin's purges would reach their hysterical peak, the Dean of Faculty who had recommended his appointment was relieved of his post for 'ideological reasons'. Bakhtin's dismissal was ordered in June of the same year because he had allowed 'bourgeois objectivism' to colour his teaching, a charge which, in the prevailing climate, might have been enough to lead to his death. Once again, however, events took an unlikely turn. Before the decree ordering Bakhtin's dismissal had taken effect, the Institute's Director, who had signed it, was himself 'exposed' as an 'enemy of the people' and dismissed; Bakhtin promptly appealed to his successor that he be allowed to leave 'of his own accord' due to the recurrence of his osteomyelitis. His plea, once again, was accepted.

Bakhtin headed for Moscow and the assistance of Kagan, and spent the rest of 1937 travelling between the capital, Leningrad and Kazakhstan, all in the vain hope of obtaining some kind of secure position. The remainder of the 1930s and the war years were in fact spent teaching in secondary schools outside Moscow. Here again, even in the face of amputation and in close proximity to the front opened in mid-1941 by Hitler's invasion, Bakhtin somehow managed to maintain what can only imperfectly be termed his 'output': he wrote, but did not publish, the materials that would later become 'Forms of Time and of the Chronotope in the Novel', 'From the Pre-history of Novelistic Discourse' and 'Epic and Novel' (which would see the light of day only in 1975); the dissertation on Rabelais that would become *Rabelais and His World* (published in 1965); several shorter pieces that would not be published until 1996; and the work on the *Bildungsroman* that would twice – perhaps – go up in smoke, leaving only a fragment to emerge in 1979. Yet Bakhtin's travails were mild in comparison to those of his co-thinkers Voloshinov and Medvedev. Voloshinov died in Leningrad in 1936 of tuberculosis. Medvedev, who in his 'worldliness and practicality' had played a greater role in public intellectual life than any other member of the 'Bakhtin Circle', became its symbolic sacrifice when he was shot in 1938.

When Bakhtin returned to Saransk after the war to take up what was essentially his first secure, extended academic post, he was just a couple of months short of his fiftieth birthday. Even then, the institute's wish to appoint him head of department foundered on the fact that, although his dissertation had been submitted in 1940, the higher degree required for appointment to such a position had never been awarded. Bakhtin finally defended his dissertation at the tender age of fifty, only to be subjected to a final humiliation. In a marathon defence conducted in an atmosphere of grim comedy, during which an exhausted Bakhtin even claimed to have revised certain of his ideas 'in the light of Lenin's teaching' – and may or may not have waved his crutches at his tormentors, shouting 'obscurantists!' in their faces – he was eventually denied the degree of *Doktor* and awarded instead the lower degree of *Kandidat*.

This would not be the last occasion upon which the official culture would exert its influence on the ageing former exile. As the

Soviet Union began to emerge from its intellectual ice age under the influence of a number of books published in the name of Stalin himself, the effects of this changing climate on Bakhtin and society at large were extremely unpredictable. In the early 1950s, for example, Bakhtin was officially reprimanded on the grounds that his department had not been 'reconstructed' in the light of Stalin's interventions in the area of linguistics and in the light of his 'work of genius', namely, *Economic Problems of Socialism in the USSR*. The first of these, perhaps the most unlikely intervention to be associated with the person of Stalin, did, however, have a more productive, if entirely paradoxical, effect on Bakhtin. Stalin's 'Concerning Marxism in Linguistics' (1950) released a wave of renewed debate on broad questions of linguistics and the status of the literary text that had been absent for twenty years, during which the often absurd – and far from Marxist – linguistic theories of Nikolai Marr (1865–1934) had somehow been installed as Marxist 'orthodoxy'. In this environment, Bakhtin, like many others, was not only obliged to familiarize himself with the new 'Stalinist' line (Bakhtin paraphrases Stalin in notes made at around this time, and his Russian editors have acknowledged the presence of, but withheld, many further such references), but in so doing also took the opportunity to return to a line of thought and exposition that had been closed off at the end of the 1920s. The term 'speech genres', which first appeared in Voloshinov's book in 1929, returns with a vengeance and lies at the core of Bakhtin's work in the early and mid-1950s, most notably in 'The Problem of Speech Genres', which was published in Russian in 1979. The important essay 'The Problem of the Text in Linguistics, Philology and the other Human Sciences' was also produced at the tail end of this period, close in fact to the time of his formal retirement from university teaching in 1961. This marked not the end of Bakhtin's story, however, but only the point of its transition to a new and entirely unexpected phase.

REDISCOVERY AND REHABILITATION

The circumstances surrounding Bakhtin's rediscovery and the re-publication of his book on Dostoevsky are, perhaps not surprisingly, a matter of some debate; they also constitute the first example

of how the myths of Bakhtin, given life by the vagaries and un-
certainties of his biography to that point, are further problematized
through intervention from outside Russia. The original version of the
Dostoevsky book, *Problems of Dostoevsky's Art*, was certainly the
catalyst for a group of younger scholars, in the environment of
cultural 'Thaw' initiated by the new Soviet leader Nikita Khrushchev,
to seek out its author – if, indeed, its author was still alive. The
process of revising the book appears, however, to have been initiated not by Russian patriots of the younger generation attempting
to undo the wrongs of the Stalinist past, but by an Italian (and then
Communist) academic, Vittorio Strada (b. 1929), who wanted to
use Bakhtin's work as an introduction to an Italian edition of
Dostoevsky. The truth that had so often been a casualty of the
Stalinist years would fare no better in the struggle over Bakhtin's
legacy in Russia, and it would fare even worse in the process of its
transmission to the West. A revised version of the Dostoevsky
book was duly published in Russia in 1963 as *Problems of Dostoevsky's Poetics*, followed by a more extensively revised version of
the dissertation on Rabelais in 1965 and by Bakhtin's formal
'rehabilitation' in 1967. It emerged that *Resurrection* had never
really existed as an 'organization' in any real sense; Bakhtin, at
least, unlike many of the others who had been arrested on similar
charges, had the consolation of 'living through', as the Russian has
it, and of seeing himself formally absolved.

But what role might Bakhtin – or at least his work – play in the
contemporary theoretical debates to which he had been returned?
On the basis of the second part of the Dostoevsky book, in which
he utilized, critiqued and developed the language of the Formalists,
and on the basis of apparent prefigurations of Structuralism present
in his *Rabelais and His World*, Bakhtin was soon 'claimed' by the
inheritors and representatives of these tendencies. In Russia, he was
effectively claimed as a forerunner of the Moscow-Tartu School of
semiotics, a claim that was strengthened by the contention that
Bakhtin was in fact the 'real' author of Voloshinov's work on linguistics in the 1920s. In the West, where early Russian Formalism
was being 'excavated' as one of the important bases of Structuralism, and where, moreover, *Rabelais and His World* had been
translated into English (1968) and French (1970), Bakhtin became
associated from the very outset with Structuralism 'with a human

face'. Worse, from the point of view of those in Russia who had sought to salvage Bakhtin from the intellectual wreckage of Soviet Communism, the association of Bakhtin's authorship with the works of Voloshinov and Medvedev would make him an extremely attractive figure for a critical tendency even less 'acceptable' than Structuralism – Western Marxism. Marxism, in any of its forms, was more or less anathema to generations of academics who had been force-fed its Soviet incarnation. Such associations may have seemed little short of grotesque to those who would edit collections of Bakhtin's key works for Russian editions in 1975 and 1979, but they did nonetheless set the tone for Bakhtin's later odyssey in the West.

While the Western critical and theoretical environment was being exposed to a tantalizingly partial glimpse of Bakhtin's oeuvre, dominated by carnival, a broader picture of his theoretical significance was being prepared in the 1975 Russian edition of his work entitled *Questions of Literature and Aesthetics*. Before the book appeared, however, an increasingly frail Bakhtin, whose health had deteriorated markedly after Elena's death in late 1971, died in March 1975 at the age of 79. Like the Formalist critic and writer Viktor Shklovsky (1893–1984), Bakhtin was one of those relatively rare cultural and literary figures born in the late nineteenth century to have lived long enough in the Soviet Union to witness the rise, reification and (almost) passing of the centralized Soviet model of culture in its 'purest' form.

The texts published in *Questions of Literature and Aesthetics* would later form the core of *The Dialogic Imagination*, the collection that would accelerate interest in Bakhtin in the West into a veritable 'boom'. Hitherto unknown work followed in the 1979 Russian collection entitled *The Aesthetics of Verbal Art*, which included 'The Problem of Speech Genres' and, in a development that would prolong the 'boom' by challenging any received or stable perceptions of Bakhtin's work, the early philosophical essay 'Author and Hero in Aesthetic Activity'. This was followed in 1986 by *Toward a Philosophy of the Act*. These works revealed a more thoroughly 'philosophical' Bakhtin than those who participated in his rediscovery at the end of the 1950s could have imagined – and they initiated a revision of the shape of Bakhtin's thought as a whole, as well as perceptions of its points of continuity and discontinuity with various strands of Western literary and cultural theory. The story of those continuities and discontinuities would in turn give way to – or in fact *produce* – an entirely 'new' Bakhtin, one whose significance would not so much exceed the boundaries of literary studies or of literary and cultural theory, as signal the collapse of such boundaries and the emergence of a differently conceived Humanities.

It is in this context that the following expositions of the main elements of Bakhtin's thought are offered, beginning – in a manner that is highly appropriate in the context of his life – with work that was written first and published last.

SUMMARY

Bakhtin lived a difficult, unorthodox and unglamorous life, which was repeatedly disrupted by major political and cultural upheaval. The purpose of this biographical sketch was not only to convey some of the complexities – and the drama – of Bakhtin's lived experience, but also to set his published work in a context that is more than marginally important for its understanding. The process of publication – and, later, translation – of some of Bakhtin's most important texts was fragmented and disordered by political and cultural circumstances unique to the Soviet environment. Its reception outside Russia has therefore been defined in large part by discontinuity, with many of Bakhtin's contributions to what were 'live' debates at the time of their *writing* taking on a quite different resonance at the time of their *publication*. This sense of belated-ness, of coming from 'out of time' as well as from a different 'place' – it is, in effect, *doubly* decontextualized – has both inhib-ited understanding of Bakhtin's work and heightened its intellectual lustre, the sense of daring non-conformity that is inherent in many of the texts themselves – and which is an important characteristic of Bakhtin's work as a whole.

3

SELVES AND OTHERS

It is difficult to say precisely what 'type' of thinker Bakhtin was at the beginning of his career, at the point in the early 1920s when he wrote – but did not publish – two highly idiosyncratic, and therefore often quite difficult, works: *Toward a Philosophy of the Act* (written c. 1921, published only in 1986; English translation published in 1990) and 'Author and Hero in Aesthetic Activity' (written 1922–24, published only in 1979; English translation published in 1993). The closest approximation would be 'philosopher', although these works are far from conforming to the norms of academic philosophy; they are, moreover, conspicuously concerned with *literature*, which is brought into the orbit of philosophy as a specific – in fact unique – category in aesthetics. Most importantly, at the heart of these works there is a model of self-other relations that is clearly not restricted to the 'fictional' world and that is implicitly offered in description of how, to put it at its simplest, human beings understand and interact with one another. As this book unfolds, we will focus increasingly on the implications of the fact that Bakhtin's model of self-other relations, while not restricted to literature, depends at the same time on literature for its exposition.

The terms in which this model of self-other relations is expressed are the building blocks of Bakhtin's mature thought, feeding forward to the core concept of dialogism. Eventness, answerability,

embodiment, outsideness, finalization and unfinalizability, and architectonics are all indispensable to the Bakhtinian view of the world
and the text; they are also, as is immediately clear, quite unfamiliar
to those interested in philosophy as much as to those primarily
interested in literature. This chapter will outline, indeed, the basic
'architectonics' of Bakhtin's model of self-other relations, a discussion that will necessarily involve consideration of more familiar, if
perhaps no less difficult, concepts – being and the self. We are
obliged to begin, however, in what might seem a rather awkward
place for someone who has impacted so profoundly on 'theory'.

THEORETICISM AND EVENTNESS

The fragmentary opening of Bakhtin's earliest extended work, *Toward
a Philosophy of the Act*,[1] almost immediately identifies theoreticism
as one of the key ills of modern (and, in particular, scientific)
thought. Theoreticism is the name Bakhtin gives to all forms of
thought that imagine that cognition or description of what he
calls the 'content/sense' of any act exhausts its full value or significance, and the 'act' is explicitly understood as covering thoughts
and statements as much as actions. What different people may say
or do in differing situations cannot necessarily be equated in terms
of an apparently similar content or meaning, just as, for example, a
statement of legal or scientific principle, while valid within the
bounds of its own particular domain, does not exhaust the ways
and contexts in which it might have significance. This is because
the 'theoretical transcription' of the apparently straightforward
meaning that can be abstracted from the act (or thought, or statement) is never adequate to what Bakhtin calls 'the actual once-
occurrent world' (TPA 12) in which acts are performed by actual,
located subjects. Purely 'theoretical' – that is, abstract – thinking
cannot therefore access what might be regarded as the absolute
core of Bakhtin's thought: the 'once-occurrent *event* of Being' (TPA
12, my emphasis). Theoreticist (abstract) thinking will always produce a partial, limited account of its object, whether that object is
human action, speech or writing. Theoreticism will always miss the
eventness (*sobytiinost'*) of any act or phenomenon, its quality of
being uniquely located, bodily and temporally, in a subject who
consciously accepts responsibility for his or her act. Nothing can be

perceived in the fullness of its meaning if understood without regard to its eventness.

This is not a global dismissal of the content of scientific thought, the propositions of which are valid within its own particular domain: gravity, for example, acts on its object in ways that are describable and generalizable, but such description cannot – and does not try to – access the totality of *my* or *your* experience of gravity. To use an example from a slightly later work – 'The Problem of Content, Material and Form in Verbal Art' – knowledge of the chemical composition of paint is not the same as the understanding (the experience) of the impression colour makes on the viewing subject; more profoundly, technical and scientific propositions may have an intrinsic validity in the 'world of technology', but if that world is not constrained by 'laws' that are not limited to the logic of technology itself – if allowed, in other words, to pass itself off as the 'whole' of the world – it may generate dangerous, perhaps catastrophic, consequences for the world beyond technology. In broad terms, Bakhtin begins by refining the age-old philosophical problem of the 'general' and the 'particular', arguing that 'generalizable' knowledge – the law of gravity, the properties of fire – must be strictly distinguished from knowledge/experience of a specific actuality as it is perceived/experienced by a given individual at a given moment – falling, being burned.

This principle is not limited to the 'exact' sciences and is in fact even more fundamentally problematic for the Humanities and Social Sciences. In the Humanities, it may be much easier to mistake the content or 'meaning' of an act or statement for its 'signature' eventness: a philosophical proposition such as 'thought determines being', for example, although it may in its content seek to oppose static and essentialist conceptions of being, nonetheless has a tendency to imply some kind of universal applicability. It *invites* abstraction as a 'general' principle, severing itself from what Bakhtin calls the 'ontological roots of being' (TPA 44). The implications of theoreticism for the Human and Social Sciences are greater and potentially more damaging to a full understanding of the *object* of these disciplines. Although the exact sciences may be limited in the account they are able to give of their object, that account is nonetheless adequate to the terms of its own context and purpose (the chemical composition of paint, for example, or the quantum mechanics of nuclear fission). Yet, if ethics, for example, generates a generalizable principle that might become the basis for law, it necessarily does so without regard for the eventness of the individual act (or potential act) performed by an actual, embodied subject. It thus inscribes theoreticism into phenomena that will not only have a direct impact on human activity, but that are also designed for this specific purpose (unlike technology, which may indirectly affect the 'ethics' of human conduct, but whose primary function is different). Where the Humanities and Social Sciences mimic the methodological and philosophical assumptions of the exact sciences – a charge that with some justification might be laid against literary studies, linguistics, psychology, philosophy, anthropology, economics and political theory at certain stages of their development in the twentieth century – the deleterious effects of theoreticism become yet more pronounced. The Humanities and Social Sciences, in failing to understand action and utterance in terms of the once-occurrent eventness of their production by actual, embodied subjects, risk terminally *objectifying* their objects and thus failing to grasp and account for what is essential about human experience.

The solution to this crisis in modern thought is not, however, simply to turn to what Bakhtin describes as the opposite of 'scientific (theoreticist) thought' – 'aesthetic seeing'. Aesthetic seeing, a form of cognition of and orientation towards an object which admits of an emotional or even 'intuitive' element – and which might therefore appear as some form of antidote to abstract, rationalist (theoreticist) thinking – is also incapable of 'possessing' the once-occurrent event of being. Aesthetic seeing in fact produces a different kind of 'partiality' in respect of its object, this time not because, like theoreticist thought, it fails to ground 'content/sense' in an actual, embodied subject position, but because it radically *overdetermines* the non-rational, emotive aspect of its object. It has a tendency to become lost in its own object and thus to dissolve the object in an imagined version of it, the 'product' of aesthetic seeing – the image or work of art itself. This 'product' is as imperfect a basis for approach to the eventness of the performed act as theoreticist abstractions of its meaning. Aesthetic seeing occupies the other end of the spectrum from abstract, rational, scientific (theoreticist) thinking: in attempting to combat the generalization of abstract, 'theoreticist' thinking, it *over-invests* in the particularity of the particular. Aesthetic seeing is also, therefore, incapable of penetrating to the eventness of being, although Bakhtin does acknowledge that 'aesthetic being is closer to the actual unity of Being-as-life than the theoretical world. That is why the temptation of aestheticism is so persuasive' (TPA 18).

Bakhtin's analysis of being in its eventness aligns him, in one sense, with the most progressive trends in philosophy of the period around the First World War, and it is perhaps most notably informed by the particular philosophical opposition of 'culture' and 'life' proposed by Georg Simmel (1858–1918) in his development of the challenges to rationalism produced in the nineteenth century by such thinkers as Friedrich Nietzsche (1844–1900) and Wilhelm Dilthey (1833–1911). The primacy of life context and lived experience in what is sometimes referred to as *Lebensphilosophie* (philosophy of life) is a useful way of describing what will remain at the heart of Bakhtin's thinking throughout his life – although the work of another important 'life philosopher', Henri Bergson (1859–1941), is given in *Toward a Philosophy of the Act* as a prime example of the implicitly unwelcome 'aestheticization of life' (TPA 13).

In a quite different sense, however, Bakhtin's insistence on the centrality of eventness also opens up lines of association with a very different 'philosophical' tradition, namely, the theology of Christianity – and of the Russian Orthodox church in particular – which heavily emphasizes the principle of incarnation or 'embodiment' (*voploshchenie*). The central importance of Christ as a living human being, God incarnate, provides a different frame for understanding the significance of the actual, embodied subject of the event of being. It is characteristic that Bakhtin turns to the example of 'the event of Christ's life and death' in order to provide what is perhaps the best summary of his core position on the relationship between 'culture' and 'life', as well as a dramatic statement of what is at stake in the event of being's resistance to theoreticism. 'Christ's life and death' is equally inaccessible:

a. to theoretical cognition, which might grasp its content/sense, but cannot grasp 'the once-occurrent fact of the actual historical accomplishment of the event';
b. to historical cognition, which is able to reconstruct the event as historical fact, but is inadequate to its content/sense; and

c. to aesthetic intuition, which is adequate to both aspects, but in which, crucially, 'we lose our own position in relation to it [the event], our ought-to-be-position in it'.

(TPA 16)

It is far from scandalous to say that, for Bakhtin, what is true of Christ as an embodied subject, acting in the once-occurrent event-ness of his being, is also true of any embodied subject – of any human being acting, speaking and writing. 'Full' knowledge and understanding of such being – and action, and speech, and writing – requires more than 'theoretical' or 'aesthetic' (or indeed historical) seeing alone can provide. The idea of *embodiment*, as we will later see, is crucial to the central idea of eventness.

In order to establish more clearly the productive alternative that lies between the poles of 'theoretical cognition' and 'aesthetic intuition' (leaving aside an equally partial 'historical cognition'), we need to look first at the implications of a different aspect of eventness, namely, what Bakhtin calls the 'ought-to-be-position' in relation to being – the sense of obligation or *answerability* that aesthetic intuition in itself lacks.

BEING, THE SELF AND ANSWERABILITY

The rejection of theoreticism is designed to draw our attention to a misconception of *being* itself, the correction of which will require an entirely different conception of the cognizing or seeing subject from that commonly understood in philosophy to this point. Bakhtin's subject is a 'concrete', bodily person, who thinks and acts in the stream of once-occurrent events against the background of a constantly changing series of contexts. It is clear from this that he intends a philosophy of human being, thought and action that is inimical to the broad sweep of Western philosophy since Plato (429–347 B.C.) preferred 'eternal truth' to 'our transitory and defi-cient temporal life' (TPA 11), the ideal life of the mind over the external, 'real' world (which was for Plato merely a 'world of external appearance'). More particularly, it is a response and a challenge to the 'transcendental' subject of Immanuel Kant, which was, to put it simply, invented by Kant as a way of explaining how there can be both 'things in themselves' (real objects in the world that have being in isolation from any conscious perception of them) and *a priori* concepts in the mind that allow it to make sense of and *to order* the external world. Indeed, Bakhtin has been, with some justification, philosophically aligned with 'neo-Kantianism', which should be understood as a series of attempts to re-engage with Kant's philosophical agenda – and its problems – rather than as a school determined by allegiance (as noted in Chapter 2, significant neo-Kantian thinkers include Hermann Cohen and Ernst Cassirer, as well as Bakhtin's early 'mentor', Matvei Kagan).

Bakhtin's subject does not simply mediate between mind and world, or at least does so in a very particular way: the subject *acts*, performs a deed, and in so doing makes concrete and gives value to any particular form of knowledge: 'the knowledge of the content of the object-in-itself becomes a knowledge of it *for me*' (TPA 49). Being-as-event, as we have seen, is not accessible from the theoretical transcription of the performed act (its 'content/sense'), but only from the *performed act itself*, the 'historical act of actualization' of that content/sense (TPA 7) – 'for the act is actually performed in Being' (TPA 12). In the performance of such acts – which can, we must remind ourselves, be acts of thought or speech, as well as physical 'action' – the once-occurrent event of being 'is no longer something that is thought of, but something that *is*, something that is being actually and inescapably accomplished through me and others' (TPA 13).

The only 'being' that has value, that is not a false, abstracted version of lived experience, is literally *brought into being* – performed – by the subject or 'bearer' of that being in his or her interaction with objects and other people in the external world.

This 'real' life is therefore not something that passively or automatically just 'is': it requires an active commitment, in the absence of which life is lived merely as an 'empty possibility' (TPA 43). The subject of this real life, who has the ability to give value to knowledge, make it knowledge and understanding '*for me*', is not just a consciousness, but an *answerable* consciousness, who 'undersigns' his or her own action in the process of consciously performing it. To return to Bakhtin's initial opposition between abstract, rational, theoreticist thought and thought that is adequate to the event of being, the actually performed act is 'more than rational – it is *answerable*. Rationality is but a moment of answerability' (TPA 29). A refusal of this active commitment on the part of an individual subject, what Bakhtin terms an 'alibi in being', living 'by [...] passivity alone' and choosing or affecting to ignore the implications of one's unique, concrete locatedness in respect of the world verges on being a kind of fiction, a form of non-life, a condition Bakhtin struggles to imagine as an actual possibility: 'every movement, gesture, lived-experience, thought, feeling' must be rooted in my acknowledgement of my own participation in being-as-event. Otherwise, in a phrase we have already encountered, I 'sever myself from the ontological roots of being'.

I cannot exist in a world of 'contingent possibility', but am existentially obligated to 'exist in the world of inescapable actuality' (TPA 44). The individual subject eventually and inevitably comes to acknowledge and affirm the *fact* of his or her 'non-alibi in being' (TPA 40), the inescapability of interacting with the world – actively, consciously – from one's own unique and unrepeatable location. The fact of the non-alibi in being, the subject's ineluctable answerability (*otvetstvennost'*), is the category that brings experience, history and meaning together in the rich, unified being-as-event. This Bakhtin calls 'participative (unindifferent) thinking', 'an act-peforming thinking, a thinking that is referred to itself as to the only one performing answerable deeds' (TPA 44–5). Such thinking, orientated towards the world from its unique place in the event of being, is capable even of de-objectifying its object: it makes of the world 'a world of proper names, a world of *these* objects' (TPA 53). The subject – the concrete, embodied *person* – encounters in the world not concepts, nor even 'just' objects, but '*this* sky and *this* earth and *these* trees' (TPA 30). In the terms from which we began this discussion, the 'content/sense' of anything at all – the sky, the earth, a tree – depends on the *relationship* between that object and its observer – the actual, embodied subject acting answerably in the once-occurrent event-of-being. It is through this relationship that the whole of the world, from inanimate objects to scientific laws, is 'humanized' and thus acquires the fullness of its meaning.

There are two important qualifications on what might seem at first to be a philosophy of radical individualism, related, perhaps, to the existentialism later associated with Jean-Paul Sartre (1905–80). The first and most important – the role of other people – will be dealt with in some detail in the following section. The second is the problem, to which we have already referred, of how the *particular* (the individual, the event) relates to the *general* (the collective, the reiterable, history). How, for example, can observations that are valid only and definitively with regard to the particular instance, in all its non-reiterable eventness, become the basis for a generalizable understanding of any given phenomenon? How can we avoid the trap of bracketing the individual experience or understanding of something as 'merely' subjective, while preferring the broader, 'objective' truth of a situation – preferring precisely, in other words, the purely theoretical, which cannot access the eventness of being? The tendency for 'truth' to be understood only in terms of 'universal moments' – of 'that which is repeatable and constant in it' – is, consistent with the analysis of the deficiencies of theoreticism, merely 'a legacy of rationalism' (TPA 37); but what use might a thousand, potentially conflicting, 'truths' be, in everyday life as much as in law or science? This problem is never resolved 'philosophically' in Bakhtin, but, as we will see, generates a number of attempted solutions as Bakhtin and his colleagues confront it in the languages of other disciplines.

The same might be said of a related problem, the contours of which we have already glimpsed briefly: the problem of incarnation or embodiment. It is implicit that the unique 'location' of the human subject who acts in the ongoing event of being is the human body – whether it is the body of the humblest performer of the most mundane, everyday actions or, as we have seen, the body of Christ, which is not only of symbolic significance, but which also guarantees the unique authenticity of the event of a life. We may speak of a 'shared consciousness' (a world view such as scientific rationalism or Christian doctrine), but we cannot 'share' a body. From the other point of view, however, how then can we have meaningful knowledge or understanding of other embodied subjects? This problem is, once again, not (entirely) resolved philosophically, and the problems implied by the concept of *embodiment* will prove central both to Bakhtin's literary programme and his 'translinguistics' of the late 1920s and 1930s. It also, in its self-conscious opposition to the classical mind-body dualism associated with René Descartes (1596–1650), returns us to the first and most important of the qualifications to a potential radical individualism raised above. Bakhtin's conception of the located, embodied subject attempts to answer the question that Descartes raises but elides – how can we have knowledge of other embodied subjects? It is, despite its surface impression of a potentially closed 'individualism', an attempt to deal with the problem of other people.

THE OTHER

Bakhtin's subject encounters in the world not only 'objects', the material reality onto which it must impose order and meaning, but *other subjects* – other concrete, bodily and temporally located, answerable persons living their own unique and once-occurrent event of being. Bakhtin will later go on to develop the distinction between abstract, scientific thought (from physics to economics) and Humanistic thought into something more fundamental or even absolute deriving from the capacity of the object of the Human (and Social) Sciences also to 'speak'. Here, as we have seen, he ranges what he calls 'aesthetic seeing' alongside the various instances of theoretical thought, both equally incapable of grasping being-as-event, although for opposing reasons. In order to overcome this incapacity, aesthetic seeing must become a more particular and pronounced form of participative thinking, this time involving not merely an acceptance of its own non-alibi in being (its answer-ability), but also a particular form of *empathy* in relation to everything that it is not. This is expressed in terms of what Bakhtin calls 'aesthetic contemplation', which he proposes as an alternative to the pure aestheticism that is unable to access the event of being:

> An essential moment [...] in aesthetic contemplation is empathizing into an individual object of seeing – seeing it from inside in its own essence. This moment of empathizing is always followed by the moment of objectification, that is, a placing *outside* of oneself of the individuality understood through empathizing, a separating of it from oneself, a *return* into oneself. And only this returned-into-oneself consciousness gives form, from its own place, to the individuality grasped from inside, that is, shapes it aesthetically [...].
>
> (TPA 14)

Bakhtin is quite explicit in arguing that

> empathizing actualizes something that did not exist either in the object of empathizing or in myself prior to the act of empathizing, and through this

> actualized something Being-as-event is enriched (that is, it does not remain equal to itself).
>
> (TPA 15)

'Pure empathizing', losing oneself in the other, does not accomplish this miraculous 'enrichment'; what is crucial is the sense of journeying to the position of the individual other and *returning* to oneself. Any subject requires *another* subject, located in a relation of *outsideness* (*vnenakhodimost'*), in order to acquire what Bakhtin calls 'wholeness' or 'unity'; the subject, person, individuality only becomes what he or she is – in a towering paradox – under the gaze of another.

In his next substantial (but also incomplete) work, 'Author and Hero in Aesthetic Activity', Bakhtin reiterates and develops these basic positions on being and otherness, confirming in particular the critical role of the other in the constitution of the self. The subject

> must become another in relation to himself [*sic*], must look at himself through the eyes of another. [...] After looking at ourselves through the eyes of another, we always return – in life – into ourselves again, and the final, or, as it were, recapitulative event takes place within ourselves in the categories of our own life.
>
> (AH 15, 17)

The other has in relation to me an 'excess of seeing', a 'surplus'. The other sees me from a perspective and in a context in which I can never see myself: 'least of all are we ourselves able or competent to perceive in ourselves the given whole of our own personality' (AH 5).

Using a term that draws all the aspects we have discussed together, Bakhtin describes the interlocking structures of his model of self-other relations and of meaning and understanding as a 'concrete *architectonics* [...] of the actual world of the performed act' (TPA 54, my emphasis). The basic coordinates of this concrete architectonics, in a move that makes Bakhtin's rejection of a closed individualism absolutely explicit, are described in the following terms:

> All the values of actual life and culture are arranged around the basic architectonic points of the actual world of the performed act or deed: scientific values, aesthetic values, political values (including both ethical

and social values), and, finally, religious values. All spatio-temporal values
and all sense-content values are drawn toward and concentrated around
these central emotional-volitional moments: I, the other, and I-for-the-other.

(TPA 54)

The first two terms of this triad can be refined as follows: 'I'
(whenever it is not 'I-for-the-other') Bakhtin describes as 'I-for-
myself', and 'the other' must always be 'the-other-for-me'. Bakhtin's
model is 'architectonic' precisely because it is not a model of fixed,
unchanging points or entities; it is rather a model of fluid and
dynamic *relationships*, grounded only in the inescapable locatedness
of the actual human subject who stands at the heart of it – in the
once-occurrent event of his or her being. All meaning and understanding does not revolve around this model; it is in fact structured
according to the same architectonic principle: it is an effect of and
depends entirely upon the architectonics of self-other relations.

The practical, almost sequential nature of this model of self–
other relations, with its description of bodily, located subjects in an
actual process of mutual interaction, confirms that it is distinct
from the abstract, homogenized other that has come to dominate
most conceptions of otherness in the various strands of Post-
Structuralist thought. The other is not simply what the subject-
consciousness understands as being outside itself, characterized in a
series of ethnic, social and gendered generalizations, or, worse,
inaccessibly locked in the subject's 'unconscious': these are precisely the kind of 'theoreticist' abstractions that are produced by
conceiving of an act or statement in isolation from its defining
eventness. Bakhtin's other is *always* the-other-for-me, and it always
implies its imbrication in the event of intersubjective contact. And
this architectonics of the event lies at the core of what will later be
developed into the overarching concept of *dialogism*.

THE CRITIQUE OF FREUD

Bakhtin's other has nothing to do with what is sequentially sought
and repressed in the self, which, as Voloshinov and/or Bakhtin will
later argue in the 1927 book *Freudianism*, is nothing more than the
relocation of an exterior, abstractly constructed 'phantom' onto the

interior psychic space. Dismissed by one of the most prominent Post-Structuralist advocates of psychoanalysis, Julia Kristeva (b. 1941), as 'rudimentary', *Freudianism* is nonetheless a remarkably prescient and radically bold repudiation of the philosophical basis of Freud's work and influence, which expands on Bakhtin's core conception of self and other in a process of mutual construction by emphasizing its social and historical implications. The book's central contention is that Freudianism is the most significant example of the 'fear of history' that has dominated 'bourgeois' (Voloshinov is writing from an ostensibly Marxist position) philosophy from the middle of the nineteenth century. The 'unconscious' is for Voloshinov a fiction, an invention driven by a *'sui generis* fear of history, an ambition to locate a world beyond the social and historical' (F 14). Everything is in fact available to the *conscious* mind, but prevailing ideology acts to prevent what is opposed to it from finding external expression; it becomes an 'unofficial' conscious, which the subject is aware exists in a relationship of tension and struggle with its external environment. The unconscious, constructed as a means of repression of desire, is merely a way in which the subject is invited – or compelled – to delude itself. It is an abstractly conjured veil, which conceals from the subject not only the actuality of the other that confronts it, but also, in a deepening of the tragic spiral that is implied by the subject's self-constitution in interaction with the other, the essence of its own condition. Meaning is generated in the actual once-occurrent event of being and is conditioned by the architectonics of eventness – which Voloshinov later explicitly terms 'the social'. While Bakhtin has simply evoked looking at ourselves 'through the eyes of another' (AH 17), for Voloshinov the other person through whose eyes I may look comes with his or her own ideological horizons, as 'a representative of my social group, my class' (F 87) – or not, as the case may be. Voloshinov also speaks explicitly of the event as an 'event of communication', emphasizing the role of language, which is initially (almost) absent from Bakhtin's architectonics. (This conception of the relationship between language and consciousness will be developed further in Chapter 5.) Paradoxically, perhaps, it is precisely the role of language that forms the basis of a Post-Structuralist renovation of Freudian thinking in the work of Jacques Lacan (1901–81): whereas

for Voloshinov the Freudian unconscious above all abhors language because language (discourse) is definitively social, for Lacan
the unconscious is the discourse of the Other.

FINALIZATION AND UNFINALIZABILITY

The full implications of Bakhtin's architectonics of being (of action,
speech and writing), as well as the stakes involved in ignoring them,
can be focused by examining the productive contradictions implied
by the concepts of *finalization* and *unfinalizability*.[2] The effect of
grounding meaning and understanding in 'theoretical being' rather
than 'historically actual once-occurrent being', of ignoring or
denying, in other words, the constitutive force of the moments in
Bakhtin's 'concrete architectonics', is that we will 'find [...] ourselves to be determined, predetermined, bygone and finished, that is,
essentially not living' (TPA 9). Theoreticism (unfettered abstraction
and rationalism) implies for Bakhtin a kind of *death*, a loss of any
meaningful sense of what is human in the human – it *finalizes* what
in fact requires for its meaningful existence to be open, living,
unfinalizable. Bakhtin's model seeks instead to conceive of human
agency in terms of 'living historicity' (TPA 8) – of unfinalizability.
Yet we are entitled to ask how this 'living historicity', this axiomatic openness, which maintains a sense of life conceived in its
essential eventness, can be reconciled with Bakhtin's insistence on
the concrete, *embodied* nature of the consciousness that experiences
being; how, in other words, can a person, an object or a concept be
fixed, to the extent that it can be perceived or understood, while at
the same time retaining its living capacity to change or be perceived
or understood in its (unfinalizable) eventness?

This question can be approached most dramatically by first
considering not people, but *objects* in the literal sense; even inanimate objects, for Bakhtin, are never 'predetermined, bygone and
finished':

> Insofar as I am actually experiencing an object, even if I do so by thinking
> of it, it becomes a changing moment in the ongoing event of my experiencing
> (thinking) it, i.e., it assumes the character of something yet-to-be-achieved.
>
> (TPA 32)

In a rare early reference to the role of language, Bakhtin expands on this by arguing that in *speaking* about an object and thereby expressing by 'intonation' my 'valuative attitude' towards it, I draw attention to 'that which is yet-to-be-determined about it'; I turn it into 'a constituent moment of the living, ongoing event' (TPA 32–3). In fact, 'everything that is actually experienced is experienced as something given and as something-yet-to-be-determined'; insofar as I am thinking about something, it 'becomes a participant in the ongoing event' (TPA 33). The event of being is an *open*, ongoing event, and everything that is 'actualized in it', even the inanimate object of my thinking – that is, when it enters the architectonically structured field of actual experience – is open, living, *unfinalized*.

So too, the human subject:

In order to live and act, I need to be unfinalized, I need to be open for myself [...] I have to be, for myself, someone who is axiologically yet-to-be, someone who does not coincide with his already existing makeup.

(AH 13)

The subject's participation in the open, ongoing event of being is axiomatically 'directed ahead of itself toward the event-yet-to-come' (AH 16). This fundamental openness – the unfinalized, constantly evolving potential of the living subject – is not *entirely* self-driven, nor is it *solely* bestowed upon it by another subject (as is the case with the inanimate object); rather, it is maintained within the architectonic matrix of I-for-myself, I-for-the-other, the other-for-me. It is of course to some extent self-driven, self-guaranteed by the I-for-myself's *answerability*, but this in turn requires the encounter of the I-for-the-other and the-other-for-me: I am, essentially, an object for the other, albeit a particular kind of object, and my openness-for-myself is maintained and renewed by the openness bestowed upon me by the other, for whom I am 'a constituent moment of the living ongoing event'. Between us, as it were, I am insulated from falling into 'non-being', from living life as an 'empty possibility' – from being finalized, 'determined, predetermined, bygone and finished, that is, essentially not living'. As Bakhtin will put it much later: 'In the process of dialogic communication, the object is transformed into the subject (the other's *I*)' (N70 145). Human subjects can choose to bestow upon themselves and others the quality of unfinalizability, which is maintained between subjects (and between any given subject and the world) in the architectonics of co-experience, or they can choose, by act or omission, to allow 'something-yet-to-be-determined' to be reduced to something 'given'. In the latter case, they become – to borrow a phrase from the nineteenth-century Russian author Nikolai Gogol (1809–52), by way of Dante Aligheri (1265–1321) – 'dead souls' or what Bakhtin will later term 'dumb, voiceless object[s]', as opposed to 'the bearer[s] of [their] own fully-valid word' (PDP 63).

This architectonics, a kind of living idea of structure, conditions everything towards which Bakhtin would later turn his attention – language, literature, culture, all human interaction – allowing them the degree of 'givenness' that makes them susceptible of any form of study or observation, while at the same time guaranteeing their unfinalizability. Whether in the context of a 'primary philosophy', a theory of literature, or a philosophy of language or culture (or of physics or ethics), all 'objects' are thus definitively insulated from the effects of theoreticism, demanding instead to be perceived in the light of their irreducible eventness.

SUMMARY

Bakhtin's earliest work, almost all of which was not published, even in Russian, until the 1970s and 1980s, outlines a 'primary philosophy' that will form the conceptual basis for later work that is more directly focused on literature, linguistics and culture. The key concepts in this scheme are *eventness*, the sense in which being is only accessible or understandable in terms of its once-occurrent actuality as an event in which meaning and value are created by the participants; *answerability*, which describes the necessity of the subject's active participation, from his or her own unique location in being, in the ongoing event – the subject's non-alibi in being, the 'signature' with which he or she undersigns the performed act; *embodiment*, the literal and figurative expression of this concrete, unique locatedness that emphasizes that I can only participate in being as myself and that meaning depends absolutely on embodiment in a living consciousness (thus rendering all 'universal' or 'abstract' meaning secondary – at best mere generalized approximations); *outsideness*, the necessary corollary of embodiment, which describes my fundamental relationship to the other, which facilitates empathetic co-experiencing of the event of being; and, finally, the most subtly problematic of Bakhtin's core concepts, *finalization*. This, and the related concept of *unfinalizability* (or *unfinalizedness*), which guarantees my openness, my ability to become other than what I currently am in the movement of the open, ongoing event of being, will initially dominate our consideration of Bakhtin's transition from explicitly philosophical reflection to the analysis of literary texts. The term given to this system as a whole is *architectonics*, which seeks to express a sense of structure without at the same time implying static relations between predetermined and simplistically identified 'elements'; there are no elements, only persons (subjects). The architectonics of being is, finally, the necessary antidote to the *theoreticism* of modern thought, which, in seeking to universalize what is only in fact partial, limited knowledge of individual domains of human activity, from ethics to physics, will always produce a defective account of its object, one that programmatically decontextualizes and dehistoricizes it by insulating it from eventness.

NOTES

1 Bakhtin had published the brief programmatic article 'Art and Answerability' in 1919, his only published work until the appearance of *Problems of Dostoevsky's Art* in 1929.

2 The Russian term *zavershenie* is translated in AH as 'consummation', but we will prefer 'finalization'. The related term *nezavershimost'* will be rendered as 'unfinalizability' (although it should be noted that this lexical cluster is most commonly present in Bakhtin's writing in the form of 'unfinalizedness' – *nezavershennost'*).

4

AUTHORS AND HEROES

The Bakhtinian concepts introduced in the previous chapter – eventness and answerability, embodiment and outsideness, finalization and unfinalizability – are inconceivable, in the simplest sense, when decoupled from the more familiar terms we have used to describe the basic relations between subjects, namely, 'self' and 'other'. Yet, although a particular model of 'self-other relations' stands at the heart of his thought, these terms themselves are not terribly characteristic for Bakhtin. From 'Author and Hero in Aesthetic Activity', and with a force that persists throughout his work to the very end of his life, Bakhtin prefers to 'self' and 'other' the terms *author* and *hero* – which might appear at first glance to narrow, rather than extend, the scope of his 'primary philosophy'. In this chapter, we will examine the implications of Bakhtin's insistence on 'author' and 'hero', the ways in which these terms do in fact facilitate the expansion of his programme, and the concomitant shift from an architectonics of the event as such to an architectonics of 'aesthetic activity' – and of verbal art in particular. First, though, we must deal with certain contextual factors that conditioned Bakhtin's 'migration' from philosophy to literature.

PHILOSOPHY AND LITERATURE

There are several reasons why Bakhtin chose not to develop his 'primary philosophy' in purely philosophical terms, seeking instead to mediate his programme through the idioms of literary aesthetics, language and linguistics. The first reason, the impact of which extends far beyond the particular case of Bakhtin or even the context of early Soviet Russia, was the commonly diagnosed crisis of European philosophy as a whole. This can be traced at least as far back as Karl Marx's (1818–83) paradigm-shifting insistence that 'philosophers have hitherto only *interpreted* the world in various ways; the point is to *change* it' (Marx 1845/1924). The imperative to change the world was complicated by the sheer pace at which the world was itself changing, variously dramatized by the rise of Darwinism, the increasing technologization of industry, and the dawn of the era of mass communications – from the telegraph to cinema and radio. The late nineteenth and early twentieth centuries can be characterized as the age of materialism, which immediately implies some degree of secondary status for philosophy, which risked ceding its place as the primary way of understanding the world not only to the various branches of Natural Science, but also to the various new 'Human' and Social Sciences that rose to fill the vacuum implied by Marx's dictum – sociology, psychology, anthropology and political economy.

The event that caused these developments to crystallize into crisis was the outbreak of the First World War in 1914, which presaged slaughter on the European mainland on a scale that seemed to question the very possibility of philosophy as such. This is the broad context in which the young Bakhtin, unknown and virtually unpublished, confronted the same questions about the viability and use of philosophy that mark the work of his predecessors and contemporaries, such as the founder of existentialism, Martin Heidegger (1889–1976) – who would later be discredited due to his association with Nazism – as well as Simmel, Bergson and the neo-Kantians to whom we have already referred in Chapters 2 and 3.

The second reason is more local in character: at precisely the point at which Bakhtin might have sought to complete and publish *Toward a Philosophy of the Act* and perhaps develop his ideas in a similar scholarly genre, more immediate, Soviet-specific factors added a different shade of meaning to the 'possibility of philosophy'. The early years of the Soviet period had witnessed an uneasy truce between the Bolshevik authorities and those numerous representatives of the pre-revolutionary intelligentsia who had remained in Russia after 1917. Lenin, in particular, had understood that the intelligentsia, many of whom were temperamentally, if not politically, sympathetic to the revolution, would play a critical role in the development of a new revolutionary culture. The inauguration of his New Economic Policy in 1921 heralded a limited form of cultural pluralism that would persist until the late 1920s and in which writers, film directors, dramatists, critics, and academics in disciplines such as linguistics and ethnography would play significant roles in accommodating cultural and academic activities to the demands of the emerging Marxist-Leninist political philosophy. Certain intelligentsia figures were, however, more useful – and amenable – to this process than others.

As early as 1909, Lenin had published his *Materialism and Empirio-criticism*, which was not only one of the most radically uncompromising contributions to a practical materialist philosophy, but also an excoriating critique of the dominant tendency in Russian philosophy – religious idealism – and its chief living proponents, Nikolai Berdiaev (1874–1948) and Sergei Bulgakov (1871–1944). Now, in the summer of 1922, in an attempt to contain some of the risk inherent in a policy of cultural and economic pluralism – but also, perhaps, in fulfilment of a long-standing 'philosophical' agenda – Lenin pursued an alternative to internal exile (or the brutality of execution that would follow under Stalin) as a way of dealing with elements that, he judged, could never be reconciled to the aims of the revolution. Although philosophers made up only a small percentage of those intelligentsia figures and academics sent into forcible foreign exile in 1922, the vessels that carried them have become known to history as the 'philosophy ships' because of the particular symbolism of the act. The exile of the same Berdiaev and Bulgakov with whom Lenin had earlier engaged in print, as well as that of Nikolai Lossky (1870–1965) and Semen Frank (1877–1950), not only signalled the end (in Russia, at least) of the religious-idealist strand that had once dominated Russian philosophy, but also prepared the ground for an end to the possibility of *any* philosophical alternative to the 'dialectical materialism' that would be raised in the name of Marxism-Leninism as the 1920s drew to a close. This is one of the particular forms the response to Marx's call to change the world and not merely interpret it took in Soviet Russia; it also conditions the unprepossessing philosophical territory onto which Bakhtin, like many others, chose not to step.

There is, however, a third reason for Bakhtin's diversion into other disciplines and intellectual idioms. Bakhtin's interest in literary aesthetics is in fact already manifest in *Toward a Philosophy of the Act* and, in particular, 'Author and Hero in Aesthetic Activity' in ways that exceed mere exemplification. Rather than seeing 'Author and Hero in Aesthetic Activity' as embodying a 'transition' from philosophy to literary studies, it should be read in terms of their mutual determination. In fact, Bakhtin's 'philosophy' *depends upon* and finds its fullest expression in literary relations.

FROM LIFE INTO ART ...

We have already seen how Bakhtin's initial focus on empathy develops in 'Author and Hero in Aesthetic Activity' into the need to become other in relation to oneself, to see ourselves through the eyes of the other, and subsequently to 'return' to oneself as a precondition for what Bakhtin calls 'the final recapitulative event' (AH 17). This 'final' event is, of course, never quite final, but is merely a link in the chain of events that constitute thought, action and social interaction. We do this, Bakhtin contends, all the time *in life*. The problem he faces, however, is how to take this beyond the realm of contention or hypothesis ('philosophy') and provide exemplary material that will both support the contention and illustrate how precisely this process operates in a way that mere observation of life cannot. This is in fact the key to understanding the 'Author and Hero' portion of the title: to speak of 'subject' and 'object' risks contradicting the core of how Bakhtin sees the 'object', how it is 'subjectified' or infused with the evaluative intent of the subject contemplating it; similarly, as we have seen, Bakhtin is not altogether comfortable with the terms we have used to characterize the broader significance of his early work, 'self' and 'other'. Neither 'subject-object' nor 'self-other' facilitates the leap beyond observation of 'life' necessary for the development of Bakhtin's programme; that will require a concentration on the relationship between an 'author' and a 'hero', terms that should be understood both literally and figuratively.

At first glance, this might seem to risk a dangerous conflation of 'life' and 'art' (literature) – precisely the kind of 'aestheticization' of life, perhaps, that leads to the loss of the self in the (aesthetic) object (Bakhtin's criticism of Bergson). Yet, Bakhtin is happy to accept this risk: first, he is in fact convinced of the essential continuity of ethical and aesthetic contemplation. It is not the identification of 'life' and 'art' as such that is dangerous; rather, it is a failure to understand precisely how they are related. Second, Bakhtin's author-hero model will later facilitate the demonstration of how life and art can be *differentiated* in his scheme.

'Life', for Bakhtin, is distinct from art and literature in that it is fundamentally *not* 'finalizable' in any sense, whereas 'aesthetic activity' implies some kind of provisional finalization. In life, as we have seen in Chapter 3, 'I need to be open for myself [...] I have to be, for myself, someone who is axiologically yet-to-be, someone who does not coincide with his already existing makeup' (AH 13). The 'phases' of life and aesthetic activity are clearly visible in the following:

> An ethical determination defines a given human being from the standpoint of what-is-to-be-accomplished [...] All one need do is transpose him [*sic*] into what is given and the determination becomes completely aestheticized.
>
> (AH 226)

In life, the contemplating subject confers upon the contemplated subject a momentary self-constitution, which does not reify, but remains endlessly open to repeated self-constitution in an endless series of shifting contexts (until, quite literally, the terminal loss of consciousness that is death): an *ethical* determination. The finite literary text, however, must finalize or consummate its objects in a manner that is not quite so 'open' (or 'infinite', as Bakhtin terms it) – the 'author' confers a 'givenness' upon the 'hero', but one which does not fix or exhaust the hero's axiological potentiality: an *aesthetic* determination, but of a quite different kind to the 'aestheticization of life' we encountered in the previous chapter. Literature, in other words, has the capacity to mimic – or, better, to *embody* – this open and ongoing process of the constitution of the self in dialogue with the other and their mutual context(s) (the event of being); it has the capacity to balance the openness of the event with the superficial demands of closure that its finite form necessarily imposes. This is not, however, to be understood as a *limitation*, but rather as the unique *capacity* of aesthetic activity in the Bakhtinian sense:

> Aesthetic creation overcomes the infinite and yet-to-be-achieved character of cognition and ethical action by referring all constituents of being and of yet-to-be-achieved meaning to a human being in his [*sic*] concrete givenness – as the event of his life.
>
> (AH 23)

In this conception, aesthetics and ethics can clearly not be entirely separated from one another, but what is most interesting is that, rather than ethics subsuming aesthetics, it is in fact aesthetics that, for Bakhtin, *encompasses* ethics: 'Aesthetic objectivity, in other words, encompasses and comprises cognitive-ethical objectivity' (AH 13). Rather than linger at the level of 'life' (cognitive, ethical), a profound act of contemplation must become *aesthetic* contemplation: 'before assuming a purely aesthetic position in relation to the hero and his world, an author must assume a lived-life position, a purely cognitive-ethical position' (AH 227).

Bakhtin's focus on self-other relations in terms of a relationship between 'author and hero' therefore points to two important aspects of his thinking. First, it implicitly privileges a particular *kind* of literary text, in which the axiological openness of both self and other 'in life' is represented in its perpetual flux and motion – but in which it is nonetheless represented, captured, accessible in a momentarily consummated or finalized condition. This becomes a privileged 'aesthetic', identifying – and privileging – a literature that is able, above all, to display the *architectonic* structure of the self-other relationship. Second, it provides a solution to a problem glimpsed at the outset, namely, the sense in which aesthetics – as a specialized branch of philosophy – has hitherto merely been assigned to a different corner of the philosophical hinterland than 'theoreticism', as unable as even the most abstract of exact sciences to grasp the whole of being in all its eventness. Bakhtin envisages an entirely different aesthetics, which is directed towards precisely those essential aspects of human experience that traditional aesthetics is incapable of conceiving: the unique, once-occurrent, embodied event of an individual's being in the direct and continual process of the encounter with another subject that is constitutive of that individual's self.

ARCHITECTONICS AND THE AESTHETICS OF VERBAL ART

The significance of the aesthetic and the central structuring importance of architectonics are elucidated on material that might seem surprising to readers more accustomed to Bakhtin as a theorist of the novel. Both *Toward a Philosophy of the Act* and 'Author and Hero in Aesthetic Activity' conclude with an analysis of the same poem by Alexander Pushkin (1799–1837), 'Parting' (*Razluka*), written in 1830. In each case, Bakhtin's aim is 'to clarify the architectonic disposition of the world in aesthetic seeing around a centre of values' (TPA 65). The poem's opening couplet is as follows:

> Bound for the shores of your distant homeland
> You were leaving this foreign land.

Even this small sample is sufficient to demonstrate that there are two active persons in the poem, two 'value-contexts': the 'lyrical hero', the subject of the enunciation, and the 'you' who is addressed (a former lover, now deceased). The second value-context, without losing its self-sufficiency, is 'valuatively encompassed' by the first, which is the context of the poem's only 'speaker', but the words are marked by what Bakhtin calls the 'emotional-volitional tone' of *both*: the 'homeland' is her homeland, not his; conversely, the fact that it is 'distant' is toned primarily from *his* point of view. That she is 'leaving', similarly, is marked by *his* emotional-volitional tone (she is not 'returning', which would imply her own perspective), but the land that she is leaving can only be 'foreign' from her point of view – the word is 'hers', it is intonated from her 'value-centre', even though she does not speak it. What is ostensibly the 'lyric' expression of the lyric hero is thus marked by the emotional-volitional tones of *two* consciousnesses in active contemplation of one another, without the slightest need for surface 'formal' markers of the distinction between them. From the very beginning of his career, Bakhtin provocatively insists that even lyric verse is, in Pushkin's hands at least, and in a term to which we will return, *double-voiced.*

There are, however, more than two consciousnesses present in this and indeed in any literary text. Both value-centres, that of the lyric hero and that of his addressee, are encompassed by the 'unitary – properly aesthetic – axiologically founding context of author and reader' (AH 212) – once again without losing their own self-sufficiency. The intra-textual relations between speaker and addressee, between their 'value-centres', are part of a matrix that is also composed of relations between the author and the event of the intra-textual encounter and, on the far side, an implied relationship with a reader – who will bring to the open eventness of the whole his or her own value-context.

The first point to be made in relation to the author – we will return to the question of the reader – is entirely uncontroversial, conventional, even, in the context of literary criticism: although the author as subject may often, especially in lyric, come close to coinciding with the 'author-*hero*', the lyric hero who speaks within the poem, their coincidence can never be complete. The author-as-*artist* and the author-as-*hero* (the lyric hero who speaks in the poem) occupy axiological contexts that are as distinct as those occupied by the lyric hero and his addressee in the poem. Bakhtin's point here is not simply, however, to insist that it is not the author who speaks 'directly' in the poem, but rather that what distinguishes the author as such from the other value-contexts (heroes) is his *outsideness* with regard to 'the inner architectonic field of artistic vision' (AH 212). It is only from a position of radical outsideness that the process of contemplating, empathizing and 'returning' to the self that is a condition of finalization can be accomplished, that the architectonic structure of the event of the encounter of the poem's heroes can be understood and represented in all its once-occurrent uniqueness: 'the fact that the object of empathizing and seeing is *not* I myself – makes possible for the first time the aesthetic activity of forming' (TPA 67). Just as the lyric hero occupies a position of outsideness in relation to his addressee in the poem, and they thereby participate in a process of 'forming' one another, the author occupies a position of yet more radical outsideness in relation to the inner relationship, 'the inner architectonic field' – and is thereby able to give form to the whole. An 'aesthetic reaction [of an author] is a reaction to another reaction, a reaction not to objects and to meaning in themselves, but to objects and meaning as they are for a given human being [the hero]' (AH 222). The 'inner' reactions of the heroes to one another constitute an *event*, the complex object of the 'outer' aesthetic contemplation of the author, who is able to render it in all its architectonic fullness only from a position outside of it – and in so doing creates an event of properly aesthetic activity.

The radical nature of Bakhtin's architectonics of aesthetic activity, here described on the material of lyric poetry, can perhaps be dramatized in comparison with the concept of 'negative capability' commonly associated with the Romantic poet John Keats (1795–1821). Keats also seems to privilege a version of 'outsideness' by conceiving of poetry (and art in general) in terms of the transcendence or negation of the self, the ability of the poet – and the lyric hero – to journey beyond their own subjective position, to be 'other' in relation to their own self. Negative capability is partly a response to the earlier Romantic William Wordsworth (1770–1850), whose poetry Keats characterizes in terms of what he calls the 'egotistical sublime', implying the identification of author and lyric hero, the domination of the poem and everything to which it refers by the authorial self (the stereotype that has in fact tended to dominate conceptions of the lyric). In Keats' best-known poem, 'Ode to a Nightingale', the lyric hero does not encounter or address another person, but wishes that his own self might 'dissolve,' so that he can somehow occupy the conscious position of the nightingale ('outside' humanity, 'in' nature):

> Away! away! for I will fly to thee,
> Not charioted by Bacchus and his pards,
> But on the viewless wings of Poesy,
> Though the dull brain perplexes and retards.
> Already with thee! tender is the night

Yet there remains only one value-context, only one determinant of the 'emotional-volitional tone' of the language; 'here' and 'there' in the poem are not specifically evaluatively marked (as pertaining to the speaker and addressee of Pushkin's 'Parting', for example), but are rather markers for the human and non-human world, for the self and its negation ('dissolve'), merely 'here' and 'not here'; the 'warm South' referred to in the second stanza is also 'no one's', merely a metaphor for wine, equivalent to the invocation of Bacchus, above. The 'inner architectonic field of artistic vision' (AH 212) is here not in fact a field; it is reduced (almost) to a concentrated point, comprising the lyric hero's encounter with his own 'not self', rather than an encounter with an other. Similarly, the space between the author-as-*artist* and the author-as-*hero* (the lyric hero who speaks in the poem) is a space of convention alone, reduced almost to the point of identification. Overall, we remain at only one small remove from the 'egotistical sublime', and far from the expansive and inclusive architectonics of reactions to reactions and events within events through which Bakhtin characterizes aesthetic activity.

ARCHITECTONICS AND FORM

Despite the absence of surface 'formal' markers of the change in value-context or emotional-volitional tone we referred to above, it is important to emphasize that architectonics also denotes, precisely, *form* – but form conceived in terms of the 'deep' structural relations between value-contexts, between consciousnesses other than those of the author, rather than as a purely surface phenomenon observable in the fabric of a given text. These surface phenomena, conventional formal properties, are not, however, negligible, but are *also* conceived of as subject to the value-context(s) of the participants (heroes) or creator (author) of the aesthetic event. The iambic trimeter characteristic of Greek tragedy, for example,

> imparts a certain unity of tone to all the utterances [of the characters] [...] expresses a reaction to another reaction – the author's unitary and uniform, purely formal-aesthetic reaction to all of the contending realistic reactions of the heroes, to the whole tragic event in its entirety – and thus aestheticizes that event, i.e., extracts it out of reality (cognitive-ethical reality) and frames it artistically.
>
> (AH 216)

Iambic trimeter, conventionally regarded as a self-sufficient formal element characteristic of tragedy, becomes for Bakhtin a moment of *architectonic* form. In fact, *everything* in the aesthetic work is a moment of architectonic form: theme, plot, irony, satire – all are chosen, manipulated, *present* in the work in their interrelatedness with the value-contexts of author and heroes. It is thus – and not, in some 'purely' formal manner, abstractly conceived – that they are present in the architectonics of the aesthetic event. Hence, to put it at its simplest, it is inadequate to describe both 'Parting' and 'Ode to a Nightingale' as 'lyric', to make observations about the characteristics of Pushkin's and Keats' respective poetic line, or to identify use of metaphor and allusion – unless all of these are understood as significant, but secondary elements within the architectonic field of vision.

It is difficult to isolate and order the implications of architectonics for verbal art, so numerous and fundamental do they turn out to be. One immediate implication is the axiomatic *inseparability* of 'form' and 'content': 'the concrete human being is both a formal and contentual principle of aesthetic seeing – in their unity and interpenetration' (TPA 64). Just as the 'content-sense' of an act is inseparable from the 'once-occurrent event of Being' (TPA 12), so too must all formal aspects and elements of content in the aesthetic work be considered to be mutually determinant: when Bakhtin speaks of the 'theme' of a given work, for example, he makes the disarmingly simple point that 'the same theme (its cognitive-ethical side) could be differently incarnated through a different hero, placed in a different position in relation to the author' (AH 224) – but would thereby no longer be the 'same' theme: 'one should begin an analysis with the hero, and not with the theme. Otherwise, we may easily lose the principle of the incarnation of a theme through a human being as a potential hero' (AH 229). Theme, like any other element of the artistic work, is contingent upon the architectonic dynamics of the event structured around the value-contexts of its heroes, as aesthetically finalized by its author.

This idea is underscored and extended by Bakhtin's almost casual recognition that the author is not the only consciousness that occupies a position of radical outsideness in relation to the heroes of the aesthetic event – and is not, therefore, the only 'creator of form' (AH 212). The *reader*, too, is external to the value-contexts of the heroes, to the 'inner architectonic field of artistic vision' (AH 212); the reader brings his or her own 'axiologically founding *active* ["properly aesthetic"] context' (AH 212) to bear on this field – and s/he, too, 'encompasses' the value-contexts of the heroes, integrating and shaping the event of their being 'into one concrete architectonic whole' (AH 212) – no less than the author. The formal element created or selected by the author – iambic trimeter, direct speech, etc. – is thus secondary to the *architectonic* form created by both author and reader; that the reader, who plays no role in the *composition* of the work, can be the subject-creator of aesthetic activity to no less an extent than the author is the most eloquent expression of Bakhtin's valorization of architectonics over mere 'compositional' or 'surface' form.

This insistence on the primacy of deep, architectonic form over surface, compositional form, which will be a key factor in Bakhtin's writings throughout his career, does not, however, imply a disregard for the conventional and familiar genres or modes of literary production. Just as the specific or isolated formal element becomes subject to the dynamic of the architectonic event (the encounter of the value-contexts of author and heroes), so too, at a more general level, are modes of literature – drama as such, tragedy, lyric poetry, narrative prose – either *conditioned* by the dynamics of architectonic form, or variously *receptive* to its embodiment and aesthetic presentation. In what Bakhtin calls 'pure' lyric (a category to which, he insists, Pushkin's 'Parting' does not quite belong, though Keats' 'Ode to a Nightingale' may be a closer approximation), it may seem that the author 'is absent, that he merges with the hero or, conversely, that there is no hero and only the author is present'; yet, even here 'in every word one can hear a reaction to a reaction' (AH 218), although the lyric form often leaves such reactions 'insufficiently developed' (AH 223). The architectonic profile of lyric, however, is fundamentally different from that of narrative epic, in which the indirect speech of the heroes must at times dominate the emotional-volitional tone of the whole, mediated only by the author's ability to express, 'in the tone of the transmission, his own relationship to the words of the hero, [...] e.g., ironically, with surprise, enthusiastically, in a profoundly calm epic tone, etc.' (AH 217). Similarly, in biography the architectonics of the author's aesthetic contemplation of the subject of the biography and the people around him or her may be very clearly discerned; but even in autobiography, where, somewhat as in lyric, the hero 'coincide[s] *as a human being* with the author *as a human being* [...] the hero of a work can never coincide with the author – the *creator* of that work, for otherwise we would not get a work of art at all' (AH 222). Even in auto-biography, the event of the encounter between author and hero has a subtle architectonic profile: even here, 'the *I-for-myself* (my rela-tionship to myself) [does not] represent the organizing, constitutive moment of [architectonic] form' (AH 151).

... FROM ART INTO LIFE

Bakhtin's model of the architectonics of the event, then, has pro-found implications for literature and aesthetics, which will dom-inate the remainder of Bakhtin's own life. It has, if anything, even more profound implications for our understanding and perception of 'life' itself, which cannot be said to be 'outside' of art and lit-erature in any meaningful sense. Art and life emerge as fundamen-tally, even radically, *interdependent*. And this interdependence can be approached and understood in two particular ways. First, in terms of the perhaps paradoxical sense in which it is *only* through aesthetic activity that the self-other relations of the 'life event' can be accessed in their interdependent and interpenetrative unity: art, and literature in particular, facilitate a kind of privileged access to the 'event of being', reprocessing it as the 'consummated [finalized] event of a particular life' (AH 230). Bakhtin will later rephrase this important point in his insistence that literature – and the novel in particular – represents a 'laboratory of creation',[1] in which the architectonics of the event can be viewed under conditions of artistic, but not actual, finalization.

In life, we may be located in a position of outsideness in relation to the other with whom we interact – through contemplation, empathy, before the 'return into oneself' (TPA 14) necessary for the provisional 'objectification' of the other. But we are not located outside that process of interaction in its entirety, as the author is in the literary process. In the first case, the self-other relation is 'lived', experienced; this, too, involves a degree of aesthetic activity, but aesthetic activity cannot be the dominant of lived experience without the loss of its crucial sense of concrete actuality, its once-occurrent uniqueness. In the second case, the literary apprehension of a self-other relation in which the author participates only as author (or in which the reader participates only as reader), aestheticization takes place – necessarily takes place – without aestheticizing the concrete, actual, lived, once-occurrent experience of the protagonists of that self-other relation, the heroes of the literary work. The function of art and literature, Bakhtin comes close to saying, is to move in and out of 'life', finalizing and representing the lived event in its architectonic complexity (a combination of structure and flux); only through art – or, better, aesthetic activity – can lived experience be apprehended in the fullness of both its content-sense and its fundamental eventness.

The second way in which the interdependence of art and life can be understood has even more radical implications and concerns not the 'inner field' of human experience as such, but rather the nature of our understanding of what occurs in 'life' or in 'the world' that is *not* ostensibly centred on human experience. In the text of 'Author and Hero in Aesthetic Activity', Bakhtin in fact introduces his analysis of Pushkin's 'Parting' with a quite remarkable passage that ranges across nature, geography and history, and invokes even the science that appeared to have been consigned to the dustbin of 'abstract', 'theoreticist' knowledge at the outset of *Toward a Philosophy of the Act*. Geography, for example (and in a somewhat unexpected parallel with 'Ode to a Nightingale'), knows 'no far and near, here and there; it is devoid of any absolute axiological standard within its chosen totality (the earth)' (AH 208). History, similarly, 'knows no past, present, and future; it knows no long or short time, no "long ago" or "recently" – as absolutely unique or non-convertible moments' (AH 208). In each case, this is because the only 'axiological standard' or 'centre of value' that can imbue such concepts – or indeed any thought – with meaning is the *finite (mortal) human being*. 'History and geography', therefore, 'are invariably aestheticized to a degree' (AH 208); in other words, the knowledge they produce, even the most apparently 'technical', 'empirical' knowledge ('distance', for example) must be structured architectonically, referred to the life experience of actual, concrete human beings. To return to Pushkin's poem, 'Russia' and 'Italy' are names for geographical, national or cultural entities, but they become 'distant' or 'foreign' or a 'homeland' only in the architectonically structured field of human interaction. 'From the physico-mathematical point of view', Bakhtin continues, 'the space and time of a human being's life constitute no more than negligible segments of one infinite time and space' (AH 208); science, as we saw in *Toward a Philosophy of the Act*, may produce theoretical judgements and empirical data that are perfectly valid within the domain of science, but they acquire *meaning* only when brought into the axiological field of the human – or, to put it more accurately, of concrete, embodied human beings. Thus, even the word 'negligible', Bakhtin insists, 'already possesses an aesthetic meaning' in this context (AH 208). The theoretical frame of science cannot relate 'negligibility' to the infinity of space and time; only human consciousness, aware of its own finitude, its limitation, can conceive of *itself* as 'negligible'. Scientific consciousness, too, is not entirely insulated from *aesthetic* contemplation.

This last point can be illustrated by returning to Pushkin's 'Parting', in which the lyric hero recalls the 'terrible anguish of parting' and renders his lover's attempts to placate him as follows:

You said: 'On the day of our meeting
In the shade of olive trees
Beneath an eternally blue sky,
We shall once more, my beloved, unite our kisses of love'.

Bakhtin's commentary insists that

Nature also participates in this whole, participates in the event that this whole constitutes. Nature is animated here and brought into the world of human givenness [...] the eternally blue sky – the sky's eternity is correlated in terms of value with a human life that is determined (delimited).

(AH 214–15)

The determined and delimited nature of human existence is emphasized by the fact that the lover is now dead and the reunion will never take place: there will be no kiss 'beneath an *eternally* blue sky'. And yet:

In correlation with the 'bodied' or consolidated time of human life, artistic time and space, nonconvertible and stably architectonic, acquire an emotional-volitional tonality and include [...] eternity and extratemporality, [...] and infinitude.

(AH 208–9)

As Bakhtin will later write, even the sun, while remaining physically the same, has changed because it has begun to be cognized by the witness and the judge' (N70 137). Time, space, matter – the proper objects of an abstract, theoretical knowledge – acquire meaning only in the frame of 'human givenness'; understanding of these, too – of 'eternity', even – must be architectonically structured *in the same way* as understanding of the 'lived experience' of the event of life. Aesthetic activity, aesthetic contemplation, is a *universal* of the process of human understanding. It is more clearly and more extensively apprehensible or 'visible' in the domain of art; but it is present, and necessary to understanding, also 'in life' – and in all specialist domains of life, including the ostensibly 'theoretical' domains of science and technology.

SUMMARY

The narrowly philosophical idiom of Bakhtin's earliest work gives way in 'Author and Hero in Aesthetic Activity' to the implication that literature and literary study are necessary for the elucidation of Bakhtin's philosophical programme; philosophy is not so much displaced, however, but harnessed to a very particular kind of literary investigation – which has immediate consequences for Bakhtin's implicit and explicit conception of how the Humanities in general should be approached and understood. Bakhtin's expression of his model of subject-object or self-other relations in terms of the relationship between an *author* and a *hero* also further illuminates his conception of the relationship between literature (art) and life, and in ways that deepen our understanding of the concept of unfinalizability. If the event of being is definitively unfinalizable 'in life', literature (or a particular kind of literature) is able to appear to finalize its objects provisionally or contingently, without fixing or exhausting them in ways that are inimical to or 'cancel' their eventness. This is for Bakhtin a privileged aesthetic, which subsumes, without destroying, the ethical dimension of the encounter with the other – the 'unique capacity' of aesthetic activity in Bakhtin's terms. This new form of literary analysis seeks to discern in the text the architectonics of the event, the relations between author and hero as 'value centres', and relations to the world of objects and ideas distributed around them. The architectonics of literary form – as opposed to 'surface', 'compositional' formal markers – becomes the core of Bakhtin's programme and will remain present in and definitive of each subsequent phase of its development.

NOTE

1 This appears in a brief note, as yet unpublished in English, entitled 'K stilistike romana' ['Towards a Stylistics of the Novel'].

5

TRANSLINGUISTICS

We have emphasized from the outset the extent to which Bakhtin's later contributions to literary and cultural studies emerge from and at the same time develop the models outlined in his earlier philosophical work – an insistence, in other words, on *continuity*. One of the central purposes of this book is in fact to foster understanding of more familiar concepts, such as carnival and heteroglossia, by setting them in the context of the less familiar (for example, eventness and unfinalizability). It is also important, however, that emphasis on continuity does not come to imply too strongly a static, unchanging quality in Bakhtin (as many commentators have concluded), namely that, in a sense, everything is 'there' from the very beginning. That would, as we have already come to see in outline, be contrary to the central motive force of his thought, which conceives of thought and meaning in their live, evolving, eternally open eventness – 'dialogically', as we will later term it.

In fact, in many respects the later Bakhtin is unrecognizable in both the idiom and thematic concerns of *Toward a Philosophy of the Act* and 'Author and Hero in Aesthetic Activity'. The key, if not exclusive, reason for this is that something fundamental happened to Bakhtin and his thought during the course of the 1920s as a result of factors that were both general and at the same time intensely personal. Bakhtin's early thought everywhere implies the need for – and hence dramatizes the absence of – a theory of language. Against the background of European thought's increasing concern with the problem of language, such a theory emerges – but in works published by Valentin Voloshinov, Bakhtin's friend and colleague from his time in Nevel and Vitebsk. Yet what has come to be known as the 'Bakhtinian' theory of language (discourse), emerging from an unrecoverable process of dialogic exchange between Bakhtin, Voloshinov and the broader intellectual environment, immediately sets itself not in the mainstream of thinking about language, but on its margins, subjecting linguistics and the philosophy of language to the same anti-theoreticist critique that had originally been directed at the generally abstract tendencies of all rational, 'scientific' thought. The terms and significance of Bakhtin's theory of language will form the main focus of this chapter; first, however, we will briefly examine the circumstances from which it emerged.

BAKHTIN, VOLOSHINOV AND THE LINGUISTIC TURN

One of the effects of the 'crisis of philosophy' we identified in the previous chapter has come to be known as the 'linguistic turn', which is manifest both in philosophy itself (in the work, for example, of Ludwig Wittgenstein, 1889–1951) and in the rise – and transformation – of the discipline of linguistics. The basis for linguistics as a discipline at the end of the nineteenth century consisted in a broadly ethnographic approach, pursuing the comparative study of different languages in their historical development. The early part of the twentieth century, in Russia and elsewhere, saw the gradual emergence of a Formalist approach to language, which sought to understand a given language – and language in general – as a system composed of fixed and variable elements, and which therefore shifted its focus from historical development to the internal 'logic' of language as a system. Ferdinand de Saussure's *Course in General Linguistics*, published posthumously in 1916, represents the point at which the new formal (or later 'structural') linguistics began to achieve pre-eminence and became the catalyst for the emergence of linguistics as a 'science' in itself. Saussure's *Course in General Linguistics* also exerted a huge influence on linguistic theory in Russia, which had already developed in a broadly Formalist direction in the work of Filipp Fortunatov (1848–1914) and Jan Baudouin de Courtenay (1845–1929), a tendency that accelerated after 1915 and the founding of the Moscow Linguistic Circle (whose members included Roman Jakobson, 1896–1982).

Saussure would also have a less direct, but no less profound, impact on literary studies in the latter part of the twentieth century, providing, in his definition of the linguistic sign, a key model for the study of literature through the methodology of linguistics – and, inadvertently, the basis for Derrida's literary-philosophical deconstruction. Such cross-fertilization between literary studies and linguistics became a fact of intellectual life in Russia much earlier: by the early 1920s, through creative interaction between the Moscow Linguistic Circle and a group of predominantly literary scholars from St Petersburg/Petrograd/Leningrad known as *Opoiaz* (The Society for the Study of Poetic Language), overtly linguistic approaches to the study of literature – and indeed many other social and cultural phenomena – had become a significant, if not dominant, trend. A loose alliance between the linguist Jakobson and the literary scholars Iurii Tynianov (1894–1943), Viktor Shklovsky (1893–1984), and Boris Eikhenbaum (1886–1959) pursued, at least in its earliest phase, the implications of a specifically 'poetic language', memorably summarized in Jakobson's definition of poetry (literature) as 'language in its aesthetic function' (Jakobson 1979: 305). The 'Formalist' idea that a literary work could or must be approached fundamentally in terms of its linguistic profile, from its linguistic 'style' to its rhythmic patterns, was a powerful counterforce both to more traditional forms of literary scholarship, which tended to view the work primarily in terms of the psychology of its author, and to the nascent and only very roughly Marxist approaches favoured by the Soviet government, which sought to emphasize the social provenance of the individual literary work and the social function of literature in general. Language and linguistics increasingly occupied not only some of the territory that had been vacated by philosophy as such, but, in so doing, threatened also to revolutionize the study of literature.

It is notable in this context that Bakhtin, in the process of his own transition from philosophy to literature, initially resisted the claims of linguistics. At around the time he was 'completing' 'Author and Hero in Aesthetic Activity', Bakhtin mounted a strong critique of Formalism in literature and linguistics in his (at the time) unpublished work 'The Problem of Content, Material and Form in Verbal Art' (eventually published in Russian in 1975 and in English translation in 1990). There are two main points in this critique. The first point is the danger that linguistics seeks to *replace* aesthetics, to subsume literary analysis entirely in its own methodologies. This is exemplified by the major Formalists to whom we have referred, but more powerfully by the linguists Viktor Zhirmunskii (1891–1971) and Viktor Vinogradov (1895–1969), who in fact regarded literary Formalism as a relatively *weak* instantiation of what linguistics might do for literary study. As Bakhtin writes,

> poetics clings tightly to linguistics, fearing to take more than a single step away from it (in the case of the majority of the Formalists and of V.M. Zhirmunskii), and sometimes even directly striving to become only a division of it (in the case of V.V. Vinogradov).
>
> For poetics, as for any specialized aesthetics, in which it is necessary to take account of the nature of the material (in the present case – verbal) as well as general aesthetic principles, linguistics is of course necessary as a subsidiary discipline; but here it begins to occupy a completely inappropriate leading position, almost precisely the position which should be occupied by general aesthetics.

(PCMF 261)

The second point is that linguistics is condemned for its fundamentally *abstract* character, for conceiving of language (not to mention literature) in terms we may borrow, once again, from *Toward a Philosophy of the Act* as something 'determined, predetermined, bygone and finished, that is, essentially not living' (TPA 9). But the main thrust of Bakhtin's point is clear: linguistics in general – and abstract linguistics in particular – is *subsidiary* to aesthetics, it is no more adequate to the Bakhtinian conception of 'aesthetic activity' than any of the 'theoreticisms' dismissed in *Toward a Philosophy of the Act*.

It is in work published under the name of Voloshinov, however, that the first of Bakhtin's objections to the rising imperialism of linguistics is substantially refined, and the second is developed into a full-scale alternative to the claims of formal linguistics. In the article 'Discourse in Life and Discourse in Poetry' (1926) and, particularly, the monograph *Marxism and the Philosophy of Language* (1929), Voloshinov not only constructs the basis for a higher linguistics of what he terms 'living language' (MPL 293), he also 'translates' elements of Bakhtin's earlier philosophical model of self-other relations (architectonics) into a new idiom. We should note in passing that it is entirely immaterial whether this is viewed primarily in terms of Bakhtin's theory giving rise to Voloshinov's (socio)linguistic model, or Voloshinov imbuing the earlier theory with an element it crucially lacked; either way, and whatever the mechanics of the authorship process, these works represent the creative and immensely productive encounter of two distinct consciousnesses – and are therefore fitting embodiments of the *dialogic* theoretical position they express.

SAUSSURE (1857–1913)

Saussure's *Course in General Linguistics* (1916) has a more problematic provenance than even certain works of Bakhtin, having been composed from lecture notes taken by his students Charles Bally and Albert Sechehaye and published three years after his death. It has nonetheless bequeathed three central principles to subsequent linguistic study, each of which was important in a *negative* sense for Bakhtin and Voloshinov. First, and most fundamentally, it proposes a conceptual differentiation between language as such (*langage*), a given language system or national language (*langue*), and language in practical use, commonly acts of speech (*parole*). Saussure's conclusion from this is that only *langue*, a system of norms, can be the object of a scientific methodology, while isolated and heterogeneous acts of speech (*parole*) must be regarded as secondary. Saussure does emphasize the social nature of language, but locates this also as an aspect of *langue*. For Saussure, *parole* cannot be the primary object of linguistics. Second, Saussure names this science 'semiology' – the study of signs – and proceeds to outline a theory of the (verbal) sign, which is composed of two inseparable parts: the 'signifier', the word or sound used in language, and the 'signified', the concept it signifies. What the whole sign refers to, the object or phenomenon in the real world, such as a cat or death or speed, Saussure terms the 'referent' – but insists that the relationship between the sign and its referent exceeds the scope of linguistics, thereby imposing a further limitation on its ability to engage with the social. Third, Saussure not only insists on the distinction between *diachronic* analysis of a language in its development over time and *synchronic* analysis of a given language system at a given point in time, he also insists, consistent with his valorization of *langue* over *parole*, that it is language as a synchronic system that must be the primary object of linguistic study.

Voloshinov's critique is structured around the identification of two opposed – and fallacious – tendencies in linguistic theory. *Individual subjectivism*, which originates in the work of Wilhelm von Humboldt (1767–1835) and is continued by Karl Vossler (1872–1949), holds that language is essentially a product of the individual consciousness, a creative expression; language as 'system' is here a secondary construct, merely a codification necessary for study. On the other hand, *abstract objectivism* insists that language is 'a fixed system of normatively identical linguistic forms', subject to objective laws, in relation to which individual speech is a more or less contingent variation (MPL 270). Voloshinov is principally concerned with the latter of these tendencies, which had come to dominate both Russian and Western thinking on language, largely because of the systematic clarity with which it had been imbued by Saussure, its most visible proponent. Saussure's theory had confirmed abstract objectivism's assumption of the primacy of 'understanding' over 'speaking' (MPL 272) and the essentially *passive* relationship of the speaker to the language in which he or she speaks (MPL 274). Voloshinov, without falling back into the trap of conceiving of the speaking person as an entirely autonomous individual who merely expresses his or herself through language (individual subjectivism), insists that the 'subjective consciousness of the speaking person does not in any sense work with language as a system of normatively identical forms', because such a system is essentially an *abstraction* (MPL 281). He seeks to oppose to this abstraction a sense of language as a concrete, historical, social practice, which he variously refers to as simply 'speech interaction' (MPL 312–13) or 'the living, becoming reality of language' (MPL 298) – or simply 'the word' (*slovo*). The abstract, 'closed system' of language (MPL 271) is countered with a conception of 'living historical understanding', of 'living language' (MPL 293–4). This conception of language has four key and inter-related aspects, each of which responds in some way to Saussure and the assumptions of abstract objectivism: a theory of the *utterance* as the fundamental unit of (trans)linguistic study, as opposed to the formal units of language as conceived by linguistics (from the phoneme to the sentence); a theory of the *social*; a theory of the *sign*; and, finally, a theory of *consciousness*. We will examine each of these four elements in turn, signalling the ways in which Voloshinov's theory restates and re-orientates Bakhtin's architectonics of self-other relations – and their implications for literature – as we go.

THE UTTERANCE

At the core of Voloshinov's alternative linguistics – or translinguistics – is the concept of the *utterance* as the 'true centre of linguistic reality' (MPL 278), as opposed to the units of 'abstract' linguistics, from the phoneme to the sentence. His focus is, in other words, diametrically opposed to that of Saussure: *parole* – living speech – is the primary object of translinguistics. The utterance, or 'concrete utterance' (DLDP 73), is a speech performance or act, which is determined not only by the intention of the speaker, but by the concrete situation in which the utterance takes place – and, crucially, by its orientation towards a listener, who occupies the same 'extra-verbal' context or situation (DLDP 11–12; MPL 313) as the speaker. The utterance is always '*orientated towards an interlocutor*' (MPL 301), not an imagined or abstract interlocutor, but a concrete person, who may be less or more well known to the speaker, who may occupy a higher or lower position in a social or professional hierarchy, and so on. The meaning of the utterance is therefore not determined by the abstract meaning of words selected from the language system, or by the pure expressive intention of the speaker, but by the totality of the elements – verbal and extra-verbal – present in the 'speech situation'. The form of the utterance, similarly, is not entirely determined by the speaker, but is a product of the concrete process of 'speech interaction'.

SLOVO – 'THE WORD' – DISCOURSE

English translations of work by Bakhtin and Voloshinov have had to confront the particular difficulties presented by the prevalent and critically important term *slovo*. Its simple meaning is 'word', but, given that the term is used to emphasize the principled distance between a Bakhtinian translinguistics and the 'abstract' linguistics to which it is opposed, translators have sometimes rendered it – most notably in the title of 'Discourse in the Novel' – as 'discourse', a term that enters the lexicon of linguistic study much later, precisely in order to signal the priority of language as it is practically used. 'Discourse', like the original *slovo*, is intended to signify living language, as opposed to the abstractions of linguistics.

The utterance is therefore, as a moment or instantiation of an endless process of speech interaction, immune from certain problems that pertain to the units of 'abstract' linguistics, such as the sentence, which can only relate to one another in a mechanical process of aggregation; the utterance is directly related, in greater or lesser proximity, to all other utterances: 'it is only a link in the unbroken chain of speech performance' (MPL 287). This is true of an utterance made in the course of a conversation, the formal and semantic profile of which is closely determined by the immediate speech situation and the immediately contiguous utterance that precedes the utterance in question; it is also true of an individual rejoinder in a dialogue in a literary work, which not only takes its place in a network of other utterances within the work, the utterances of other characters and the author, but also relates to and is partly determined by similar utterances in other literary works – and 'similar' utterances beyond the literary domain. The book, in fact, is for Voloshinov merely a 'printed utterance' (MPL 312) and derives its meaning and formal profile both from its *literary* context – other books, similar and different 'printed utterances' – and, like any utterance of any kind, from its 'extra-verbal context'. In both cases – in relation to the utterance 'in life' and the 'printed utterance' (literary or otherwise) – the utterance's definitive characteristic is that it is concrete as opposed to abstract, it is a moment in the 'event of being', or as Voloshinov memorably puts it, it is the 'script' of an event (DLDP 74):

> the extra-verbal situation is therefore not at all simply an external cause of the utterance, it does not act on it from outside, as a mechanical force. No, *the situation enters into the utterance as a necessary constituent part of its semantic* make-up [...] Life [...] does not act on the utterance from outside: it permeates it from within.
>
> (DLDP 12, 18)

The utterance is, in short, the medium in which the architectonic structure of interpersonal relations, in life or in literature, becomes perceptible in its eventness.

Voloshinov offers a concentrated and disarmingly simple concrete example designed to illustrate not only the implications of his conception of the utterance, but also the fatal limitations of the abstract objectivism to which it is opposed. Two people are sitting in a room: one says simply 'so!'; the other does not reply. Taken in isolation, the word 'so' cannot have any meaning for anyone not actually present as it is spoken. The 'utterance' here is artificially presented in isolation from the extra-verbal situation that determines it, which comprises, in the simplest terms, the relationship between the two parties to the conversation and the context in which it takes place. Neither a dictionary nor any level of formal linguistic analysis will facilitate access to the meaning of the utterance; analysis must in fact *begin* where the verbal utterance ends. The extra-verbal context consists in the speaker's and the listener's shared spatial horizon, their shared knowledge and understanding of the situation, and – although this will not always be the case – their shared evaluation of that situation. The parties to this minimalist conversation have in fact just looked out of the window and noticed that, although it is already May, snow has once again begun to fall. Their *shared* disappointment directly determines the utterance, although it remains, as Voloshinov puts it, 'verbally unmarked, unuttered' (DLDP 11):

> The snowflakes remain outside the window, the date – on the calendar, the evaluation – in the psyche of the speaker; but all of this is implicitly understood in the word 'so'.
>
> (DLDP 11)

The utterance *can* be regarded – for the purposes of linguistic analysis, for example – as something that can be isolated from its context, and therefore as something 'dead' (MPL 287); but this is merely an 'abstraction', which Voloshinov calls a 'finished, monologic utterance' (MPL 287), which can be regarded *as if* it is the product of a single consciousness or *as if* it is the meaningless instantiation of a purely abstract system of linguistic possibilities. Yet this is a fiction. Even the 'monologic' utterance, including the written work, *in fact* 'responds to something and is orientated in turn towards a response' (MPL 287). It cannot be isolated from its context, verbal and extra-verbal, without entirely losing its meaning. Only the verbal material of an utterance, understood monologically, isolated from its extra-verbal context, can be the object of linguistics as such. What exists beyond the utterance, but is at the same time *immanent* to it – its extra-verbal context – must also be an integral element of the object of study. And this extra-verbal context, as we have begun to see in microcosm, but in ways that Bakhtin's initial architectonics of the event does not (seek to) make explicit, is a fundamentally *social* phenomenon.

THE SOCIAL

Voloshinov goes as far as saying that the fundamental idea of *Marxism and the Philosophy of Language* is the '*productive role and social nature of the utterance*' (MPL 219):

> The concrete utterance (as opposed to the linguistic abstraction) is born, lives and dies in the process of the social interaction of the participants in the utterance. [...] If the utterance is torn from this real, nurturing ground, we lose the key both to its form and to its meaning.
>
> (DLDP 17)

In terms of the limited 'life' situation we have just observed, in which the immediate 'horizon' of the utterance is the closed space in which the participants are located, the social nature of the utterance is manifest above all in intonation – a social phenomenon 'par excellence' (DLDP 69). Intonation *'lies on the boundary between the verbal and the non-verbal, the spoken and the unspoken'* (DLDP 69) and, crucially, has a *'dual social orientation'* (DLDP 72), towards the listener, but also towards the object of the utterance – in our example, the snow, or nature, or the enveloping situation. The listener – whose role is underestimated or even ignored by abstract objectivist and individual subjectivist linguistics alike – relates to the speaker not simply as an individual, but as a representative of a social class, as someone who is closer to or more distant from the speaker, older or younger, etc. – and this, too, brings a more extensive horizon (or set of horizons) to the speech situation. This is at one and the same time an 'inter-individual territory' (MPL 225) and a definitively social territory, a set of social evaluations being embodied in each participant; the words spoken are 'a bridge between myself and the other', but also, at the same time, a bridge between the 'immediate social situation' and the 'wider social environment', which determine the structure of the utterance not from 'outside', through some indefinable process of 'influence' or mechanical causality, but from *within*. Social forces and evaluations are not extrinsic to the 'inter-individual' exchange, they are instead intrinsic in the persons and situation of that exchange. In fact, Voloshinov's theory of the utterance posits the untenability of any stable distinction between the intrinsic and extrinsic: social evaluations do not act on the speaker – or the listener, or the speech situation – from without, but are embodied and active in the utterances produced in that situation.

When the utterance in question is not produced in conversation, but is for example a 'printed utterance' such as a book, the 'dual orientation' of the speaker – that is, of the author – becomes all the more complex in that the 'object' of the author's utterance may very well be snow or nature – but will also commonly be the character or 'hero' we saw in 'Author and Hero in Aesthetic Activity' and who reappears in Voloshinov's (trans)linguistic analysis. The 'listener' of the real-life utterance becomes the 'reader' of the literary work, and the utterance is thus 'the expression of the social interaction of three people' (DLDP 72). The literary utterance is no less social than the utterance 'in life'; in fact, it is more profoundly and exhaustively social. The *verbal* context for the literary work consists of other literary works and forms, but also of the products of the critical environment and of the myriad forms of *non*-literary speech; the *extra-verbal* context, meanwhile, consists in the matrix of social evaluations that surround the author, the reader and the characters of the work, each of whom brings his or her own complex 'horizon' as a component of that context. The literary work, in staging and embodying the encounter of (at least) three consciousnesses, stages and embodies also the encounter of the social worlds in which those consciousnesses are formed: the literary work, rather than somehow detracting from the live social encounter of real people, is in fact a sophisticated mechanism for a more complex series of social encounters. It is a

> *powerful condenser of unspoken social evaluations*: each word in [the literary work] is saturated with them. And these same *social evaluations organize artistic form* as their *unmediated expression*.
>
> (DLDP 76)

The *immanently* social nature of the utterance is emphasized with reference to the literary process, in which the listener (reader) is already part of the architectonic structure of the work, an active participant in it. The listener/reader cannot be identified with the 'public' (or the 'critics'); in fact, if an author takes 'conscious account' (DLDP 83) of a generalized audience, the architectonic structure of the author-hero-reader relationship is disrupted and the work 'degrades to a lower social dimension' (DLDP 83), by which Voloshinov means that it becomes mechanically determined by an author's perception of social forces. Architectonic form determines, on the other hand, that the listener – and therefore social evaluation – is immanent in the act of expression. A *sentence* can have no architectonic profile of any kind – it is merely an abstract, formal unit of language; but the *utterance* is entirely a phenomenon of architectonic form. The difference between 'surface' form and architectonic form is never clearer than in the difference between the sentence and the utterance.

THE SIGN

Voloshinov's focus on the utterance and the inherently social nature of discourse does not imply a rejection of the significance of the sign or of the 'semiology' Saussure has proposed to build around it. Utterances are composed of signs, but not, as we might by now have come to expect, signs as conceived by Saussure, which cannot relate to the 'real reality' they mediate (nor, for that matter, to the speaking subject who utilizes them), but only to other signs 'within a closed system' (MPL 271). For Voloshinov, on the contrary, the sign, too, is both inherently social and, moreover, *material*.

This is elucidated with reference to the hammer and sickle of Soviet symbology and the bread and wine of Christian communion. These 'instruments of production' and 'consumable products', respectively, are material objects, with a particular function or place in material reality, but, when used for a symbolic or representational purpose in the context of politics or religious ritual:

> The physical thing is transformed [...] into a sign. Without ceasing to be a part of material reality, such a thing [...] reflects and refracts another reality.
>
> (MPL 221)

The sign is a part of material reality, but at the same time signifies a reality beyond itself. The sign is thus inherently ideological, in the sense of embodying a meaning that, quite literally, cannot exist without the sign: 'Where there is no sign, there is also no ideology' (MPL 221); 'where there is the sign, there is also ideology' (MPL 222).

There are many different kinds of signs – an image of a sickle is a different kind of sign from a word, for example – but all signs share a material nature:

> Every signifying ideological phenomenon is given in a certain material: in sound, in physical mass, colour, bodily movement, etc.
>
> (MPL 223)

The verbal sign, however, predominates over other kinds of signs for two immediate reasons: first, because 'the entire reality of the word is entirely dissolved in its function as a sign' (MPL 226). The word, unlike the sickle or bread, does not have a secondary or even a primary function that is not related to signification. It is a pure sign. Second, the word is what Voloshinov calls a 'neutral sign' (MPL 226). Unlike other signs, which are specialized according to

the particular area of 'ideological creation' in which they are utilized – music, sculpture, etc. – the word can perform 'any ideological function: scientific, aesthetic, moral, religious' (MPL 227).
Furthermore, the word also dominates signification in the 'vast
area of ideological interaction' that cannot be allotted to the above
categories – *'living relations'*, including conversational or everyday
speech (MPL 227). The word, therefore, in a phrase of which
Voloshinov is fond, is *'the ideological phenomenon par excellence'*
(MPL 226).

We will discuss a third reason for the pre-eminence of the verbal
sign in the following section, but for the moment it is worth pausing
on how far this position has shifted from Bakhtin's initial caution as
to the potential usurpation of aesthetics by linguistics. Bakhtin has
earlier argued, on one hand, that the situation of an author working with verbal material is 'more complex' than, for example, a
sculptor working with marble, but ultimately 'in principle no
different' (PCMF 265). On the other hand:

> Investing the word [*slovo*] with everything that comprises culture, [...]
> [we] very easily come to the conclusion that, apart from the word, there is
> in culture nothing at all, and that the scientist and the poet, equally, are
> concerned only with the word. But by dissolving logic and aesthetics, or
> even just poetics, in linguistics, we destroy the specificity of the logical
> and the aesthetic, and also, in equal measure, of the linguistic.
>
> (PCMF 291–2)

The key expression here is the closing 'in equal measure, of the
linguistic': Bakhtin rejects, that is, the ubiquity or universality of
the verbal sign as specifically conceived by abstract objectivism.
In the work published by Voloshinov, however, a detailed counter-
theorization to abstract objectivism emerges, which proposes the
universality of the verbal sign on an entirely different basis – a
theorization, as we have seen, not of 'inert' signs, but of living
signs and utterances saturated with social meaning.

CONSCIOUSNESS

That the sign is no less social than the utterance is emphasized by
Voloshinov's insistence that, in its materiality and objectivity, it is

'a phenomenon of the external world' (MPL 223), as opposed to something that is somehow formed in the mind of the speaker. This opens the way for the most ambitious aspect of Voloshinov's theory of discourse, which can be framed in the following terms: if the sign is an ideologically saturated phenomenon of the *external* world, what is the nature of its relationship to the *inner* processes of the speaker or writer who deploys it – to the process of understanding and to consciousness itself? Idealist philosophy answers this question by imagining that the sign 'is merely a shell, merely a technical means for the realization of an interior effect – understanding' (MPL 223), which is to deny all the properties of the sign we have enumerated. Voloshinov insists, on the contrary, that 'understanding can only come into being in some form of signifying material' and, therefore, that 'consciousness can realize itself and become a fact of reality only in the material of signifying embodiment' (MPL 223). Consciousness can only be said to *exist* in the material of the (verbal) sign.

Consciousness 'works', therefore, in the following way: the 'chain of speech performance' (MPL 287) we observed above runs in parallel to a 'chain of ideological creation and understanding', in which 'understanding responds to the sign – in signs', without the possibility of a break in the chain:

> Nowhere is the chain broken, nowhere does it sink into the immateriality of an inner being that is not embodied in the sign. [...] Signs arise only in the process of interaction between individual consciousnesses. And the individual consciousness is filled with signs. Consciousness becomes consciousness only in the process of being filled with the ideological, that is, with signifying content – only, therefore, in the process of social interaction.
> (MPL 224)

If consciousness were somehow to be emptied of its 'signifying ideological content' (MPL 226), precisely *nothing* of consciousness would remain. The consciousness of Idealist philosophy '*is a fiction*' (MPL 306–7), an '*asylum ignorantiae*' for all philosophical constructions. A Voloshinovian-Bakhtinian consciousness, on the contrary, is 'an objective fact and immense social force' (MPL 307). The *individual* consciousness is '*a socially ideological fact*' (MPL 225):

> Consciousness is formed and comes into being in signifying material, created in the process of the social relations of an organized collective. [...] The consciousness [of individuals] comes into being for the first time in the stream of speech interaction.
>
> (MPL 225, 297)

The verbal sign is not only 'neutral' and ubiquitous, able to perform 'any ideological function', from the scientific to the religious, it is also

> *the signifying material of inner life – of consciousness* (inner speech). Consciousness could develop only by means of flexible and corporeally expressed material. Such also is the word. The word can serve, so to speak, as the sign of internal use; it can realize itself as a sign without being fully externally expressed.
>
> (MPL 14)

Voloshinov thus insists on the definitively *social* nature of consciousness, not in an abstract or generalized sense, but at the level of the concrete individual. The verbal sign 'accompanies' not only all forms of *externalized* ideological creation, but also the inner workings of consciousness, any act of understanding or interpretation, whether or not it is expressed. Inner speech, too, is a material, social phenomenon.

How then, in a final consideration that will return us to the question of 'aesthetic activity' in the form of speech and, more pertinently, writing, does inner speech relate to 'outer' speech, to what is externalized or expressed – the utterance? How does conscious experience or understanding become expression? Voloshinov's answer is that inner speech can only be distinguished from outer speech in *formal* terms – form being understood, of course, architectonically. Voloshinov argues that different layers of consciousness correspond to different 'layers of inner speech' (MPL 93) according to their relative proximity to the point of expression or externalization: that is, the process by which speech (thought) is 'formed' is graduated, progressing towards the point where it acquires an externalized formal profile in the moment of expression. Consciousness, far from being the fiction or *asylum ignorantiae* of Idealist philosophy, is an 'objective fact' (MPL 90). In the mind of the speaker, however, thought remains 'an inner-verbal embryo of expression, [...] too small a scrap of being' (MPL 90). 'The exterior actualized utterance', on the contrary,

> is an island, rising out of the boundless ocean of inner speech; the dimensions and forms of this island are determined by the given situation of the utterance and of its audience. [...] It is not experience that organizes expression, but, on the contrary, expression that organizes experience, and for the first time gives it a form.

> (MPL 85, 96)

Consciousness is therefore conceived of as both the product and record of 'actually becoming being', as material and social as the experience of the conscious subject – and 'there is no experience outside of signifying embodiment' (MPL 85).

Voloshinov does not say it, but it is everywhere implied: the very consciousness of the speaking subject or observer, rather than being a purely 'inner' phenomenon, a ghostly but somehow fixed property, is also determined by its participation in the architectonically structured event of speech, cognition and social interaction; consciousness, too, is a moment in the architectonics of the event and must itself be understood, in its interaction with other consciousnesses, architectonically.

SUMMARY

Voloshinov's transposition of Bakhtin's model of self-other relations into the idiom of linguistics is designed to extend the range of the core Bakhtinian projection and at the same time to challenge the dominance of the Formalistic linguistics of what Voloshinov calls 'abstract objectivism', the most influential proponent of which was Saussure. The resultant *translinguistics* comprises four mutually dependent elements, each of which offers a correction to a particular blind spot or misprision of abstract linguistics: first, a theory of the *utterance* as the basic 'unit' of translinguistic analysis, as opposed to the units of formal linguistic study (such as the sentence), which are not determined by or receptive to the architectonics of the event that is encoded in the concrete utterance; second, and by extension, a theory of the essentially social nature of language, which locates the utterance at the heart of an endless matrix of social interactions which are present in varying degrees in the act and moment of speech; third, a theory of the *sign* – principally, the *verbal sign*, the word – as the material embodiment not simply of social evaluation, but of all ideology; and fourth, and finally, a theoretical definition of *consciousness* as a definitively material and social phenomenon as concrete and historical as language itself. Voloshinov's translinguistics is not simply significant as a frame for Bakhtin's later work – for which it is, nonetheless, indispensable – but, on its own radically creative terms, as a perhaps unsurpassed statement of an integrated materialist theory of language. It represents not just an enabling 'turn to language', but a turn to language on very particular, explicitly materialist terms, which insists on the concrete and historical nature of language, consciousness and ideology. Everything Bakhtin has to say about language, literature and culture from this point must be mediated, to some extent, through this all-encompassing theory of discourse and experience.

6

DIALOGISM

The contours of the central concept of dialogism are already visible in Bakhtin's early philosophical work and in the translinguistics that emerged under the name of Voloshinov; but it is in relation to *literature* – conceived translinguistically – that dialogism is given its fullest and most compelling expression. This chapter will show how the kernel of the idea that is present 'before language' and in an as yet unconsummated relationship with literature ultimately depends upon and finds its fullest expression in literary relations – initially on the specific basis of the work of Dostoevsky.

Literature, as we have seen in Chapters 3 and 4, is already a constant presence in Bakhtin's early philosophical work and is also never entirely absent from the work in which Voloshinov's particular variant on the 'linguistic turn' is elaborated; indeed, 'Discourse in Life and Discourse in Poetry' stands as a testament to the gravitational force exerted by literature, even in a work whose primary object is a putative translinguistics. The linguistic turn in Bakhtin's work might indeed confirm the shift *away* from philosophy, but its simultaneous rejection of the emergent science of (abstract objectivist) linguistics also confirms the shift further *towards* literature – and indeed substantially conditions the approach to the literary text that will dominate much of Bakhtin's later work.

This bears heavily on the sense in which 'Author and Hero in Aesthetic Activity' is 'incomplete': in its original conception, it was to close with a detailed assessment of 'the problem of author and hero in Russian literature', intended as a necessary exemplification of the work's core ideas and, perhaps, as a more fulsome treatment of the embryonic concept of dialogism. The unwritten chapter, 'The Problem of Author and Hero in Russian Literature', was instead transformed eventually into a more extended treatment of a single author from the history of Russian literature, Dostoevsky, a treatment that turned out to be no less dynamically fractured than the unfinished 'Author and Hero in Aesthetic Activity'.

DOSTOEVSKY: FROM POLYPHONY TO DIALOGISM

Bakhtin's book on Dostoevsky was originally published in 1929 under the title *Problems of Dostoevsky's Art* not long after he had been arrested; a revised edition would appear under the title *Problems of Dostoevsky's Poetics* in the distant year of 1963 (transformed in part by the appearance of a chapter on carnival, to which we will return).

The need for a degree of terminological caution is a constant in reading Bakhtin, and never more so than in relation to the Dostoevsky book, which appears to move onto entirely new ground by opening with the contention that Dostoevsky is 'the creator of an essentially new novelistic genre [...] the polyphonic novel' (PDP 7). *Polyphony* has therefore, and quite understandably, enjoyed great currency as one of Bakhtin's key terms – despite the fact that it is little more than a staging post, which quickly gives way to a more fundamental terminology. Bakhtin himself acknowledges this by emphasizing that polyphony, a musical term that indicates the presence of many voices (or parts) in a given composition, is a 'graphic analogy, nothing more' in application to Dostoevsky and literature (PDP 22). The 'image of polyphony' serves, however, to foreground 'those new problems which arise when a novel is constructed beyond the boundaries of ordinary *monologic unity*' (PDP 22, my emphasis). 'Polyphony', which is relatively clear in its own (metaphorically) limited terms, serves to illuminate the phenomenon to which it is opposed – 'monologic unity' or, simply, *monologism* and the *monological.*

At the level of the novel, 'monological' is the term Bakhtin coins to characterize novels in which all elements of the narrative – from first- and third-person narration to the indirect speech of characters – are a determination of the *single consciousness of the author.* The world of this novel – at this stage, most novels – is 'a monologically understood objectified world relating to a single and unified authorial consciousness' (PDP 9). Even where ideas are attributed to characters, where dialogue is put into their mouths, the discourse – the external expression of consciousness – belongs to the author. It does not genuinely contain the many voices implied by polyphony; all are reduced to a single voice (or consciousness) – that of the author. The world of this novel does not, in other words, conform to the 'concrete architectonics [...] of the actual world of the performed act' (TPA 54), to the architectonic structure of the event, the encounter between subjects that characterizes Bakhtin's model of self-other relations.

In drama, too, where characters on stage apparently speak in their own 'voice', the dramatic dialogue remains 'encased in a firm and stable monological framework' (PDP 17), which is controlled by and can be identified with the author. In poetry, as Bakhtin will argue in a later work, and especially in lyric poetry, 'the language of the poet is his language, he is utterly immersed in it [...] as a pure and direct expression of his own intention' (DN 285), regardless of the particular compositional structure of the poem. Both drama and poetry, despite their formal distinctiveness, are closer to the monological novel than is Dostoevsky's polyphonic novel. In monological literature of any kind – poetry, drama, or novel – the author is the sovereign subject of discourse, while his or her characters are merely *objects* of that discourse.

In Dostoevsky's novels, the 'monological plane of the novel' is fractured because 'the character is treated as ideologically authoritative and independent; he is perceived as the author of a fully-weighted ideological conception of his own, and not as the object of Dostoevsky's finalizing artistic vision' (PDP 5). Dostoevsky represents his characters not as 'images', but rather as 'ideas' or 'idea-forces'; more precisely, the idea is *embodied* in the hero/character, whom the author creates but thereby imbues with a freedom, an openness that contradicts the hero's status as a 'mere' character. In another significant echo of the architectonics of the event, Dostoevsky relates to his characters in the same way he might relate to real living beings 'in life'; his characters (heroes) are thus

> *not only the objects of the authorial word, but also subjects of their own signifying word* [...] The consciousness of a character is given as another, alien consciousness, but it is not [objectified] nor closed, it does not become a simple object of the author's consciousness. [...] A type of character appears in Dostoevsky's works whose voice is constructed in the same way as is the author's own voice in the usual type of novel. The character's word about himself and about the world is weighted as fully as the ordinary authorial word; it is not subordinated to the objectified image of the character, [merely] as one of his characteristics, nor does it serve as the mouth-piece of the authorial voice. [It is extremely independent] within the structure of the work, it is heard as if alongside the authorial word and, in a particular way, combines with the authorial word and with the equally valued voices of the other characters.
>
> (PDP 7)

The Dostoevskian polyphonic novel is not structured around 'a single and unified authorial consciousness' (PDP 9),

> it is constructed not as the whole of a single consciousness, absorbing other consciousnesses as objects into itself, but as a whole formed by the interaction of several consciousnesses.
>
> (PDP 18)

This means that it is not only *polyphonic* (because the mere presence of different character voices does not guarantee the interaction of their consciousnesses), it is also, more profoundly, *dialogic* (PDP 18):

> *The polyphonic novel is dialogic through and through.* Dialogic relationships exist among all elements of novelistic structure; that is, they are juxtaposed contrapuntally. And this is so because dialogic relationships are a much broader phenomenon than mere rejoinders in a dialogue, laid out compositionally in the text; they are an almost universal phenomenon,

permeating all human speech and all relationships and manifestations of human life, everything that has meaning and significance.

(PDP 40)

Remaining at the level of the novel, the dialogic consists in the staging of a genuine encounter of 'two or more consciousnesses' (PDP 88), which requires more than a 'mere' compositional organization of character interaction by the author; it requires a dialogical orientation, a dialogical *practice*. Moving away from the novel as such – and it is remarkable how quickly Bakhtin moves to universalize what he initially attributes to Dostoevsky as an almost unique characteristic – it is clear that Bakhtin conceives of dialogism not only or even primarily as a property of novels or of literature: once again evoking his earlier architectonics of the event, Bakhtin is unequivocal in his insistence that the author's dialogical orientation or practice in fact brings to the fore something that is 'an almost universal phenomenon, permeating all human speech and all relationships and manifestations of human life, everything that has meaning and significance' (PDP 40). All meaning is, for Bakhtin, dialogic; the dialogic is characteristic of all verbalized human interaction.

This near universal property of human interaction, Bakhtin argues, has been obscured or entirely occluded by what he calls 'the ideological monologism of modern times' (PDP 88). The monological is therefore not just a contingent product of authorial choice: Western culture, particularly in its rationalist, post-Enlightenment phase, is monological to its core and has therefore produced literature that has, in the main, been perceived as similarly monological. Dostoevsky emerges in this analysis as a kind of excavator, uncovering the submerged dialogical essence of the generation of meaning and human interaction; the 'novel' – i.e. a very particular type of novel – emerges as the medium through which this excavation can be made, revealing properties of discourse and meaning that are present in the novel, but which are also, and crucially, present (but obscured) far beyond it. Bakhtin will later attempt to demonstrate why it is specifically the novel – somewhere between the particular of Dostoevsky and the universal of 'all relationships and manifestations of human life' – that has emerged as the carrier and emblem of the dialogic.

The novel, then – or at least, for the moment, the Dostoevskian, polyphonic novel, the *dialogic* novel – demonstrates that the idea of a single or autonomous consciousness is little more than a fiction, echoing Voloshinov's characterization of the Idealist conception of consciousness – a central manifestation of 'the ideological monologism of modern times' – as a 'fiction' (MPL 306–7), which allows the 'finished, monologic utterance' (MPL 287) to be regarded *as if* it is the product of a single consciousness. Monological literature allows the elision of the multiple, socialized nature of consciousness, its apparent compression into the artifice of a 'single' or 'unified' authorial consciousness. Neither monological nor dialogical texts are functions simply of authorial choice: the former, reflecting the dominant monologism of modern Western culture, conforms to the 'fiction' of consciousness as unitary and self-contained; the latter destroys the illusion of the monological by demonstrating how consciousness, in its very mode of operation, in fact 'responds to something and is orientated in turn towards a response' (MPL 287). Consciousness, too, is fundamentally dialogical.

The dialogic novel stages the encounter of 'two or more consciousnesses' (PDP 88) in terms of the 'once-occurrent eventness' of their being we encountered in *Toward a Philosophy of the Act*. Dostoevsky is able to capture in the literary text what cannot be grasped by 'mere' cognitive activity, or even by 'aesthetic activity' as conceived by philosophy: 'Thought […] becomes itself part of the event' (PDP 10). This eventness, the 'flux of life', must remain an implicitly unknowable moment of lived experience for other forms of 'scientific' observation or analysis, and indeed for the majority of implicitly inferior literary authors (Petrarch, Dante, Heine, Rilke and of course Pushkin are other exceptions who receive honourable mention in 'Author and Hero in Aesthetic Activity'). Eventness is, however, the equivalent of the atomic substructure in Dostoevsky's (textual) world. To continue with Bakhtin's earlier terminology, the dialogic novel allows the 'finalization' – or, in more conventional literary terminology, the 'consummation' – of characters in a way that nonetheless preserves their 'unfinalizability'. Their dialogic representation in terms of their live 'eventness', their 'actually becoming being', is what guarantees the status explicitly accorded to them in the Dostoevsky book not as 'objects' of authorial representation, but as 'subjects' who relate to the author as another subject – as 'objects' who speak.

VOICE AND EMBODIMENT

Dostoevsky's characters/heroes appear as their own 'directly signifying word' (PDP 7); 'the character in Dostoevsky is not an image, but fully-weighted discourse' (PDP 52). What is thus represented in Dostoevsky's novels

> is not the defined existence of the character, not his fixed image, but rather *the final summation of his consciousness and self-consciousness* – ultimately, *the character's final word about himself and about his world.* [...] the character is the bearer of his own fully-valid word, and not a dumb, voiceless object of authorial discourse. The author's conception of the character is *a conception of discourse*. Authorial discourse about the character is therefore *discourse about discourse*. [...] Dostoevsky's character is not only discourse about himself and about his immediate surroundings, but also discourse about the world.
>
> (PDP 48, 63, 78)

Bakhtin expands on the implications of this conclusion – that 'everything that has meaning and significance' must be understood, within and beyond the literary text, in terms of *dialogic discourse* – with reference to an already familiar concept, *embodiment*, and to a new one, *voice*. The ways in which these terms are dependent on each other will illuminate a quite unique aspect of Bakhtin's thought.

If we return once again to 'eventness', to the sense in which life is lived as a sequence of unique, once-occurrent 'events of being', a strong immediate sense of the importance of embodiment emerges: human speech – all human action, in fact – emanates from a unique location, the specificity of which is guaranteed by the material embodiment of the speaker, the sense in which he or she occupies *this* specific time and space, *this* and only this location in being. This sense of embodiment is made more complex, however, by Voloshinov's insistence that '*consciousness can realize itself and become a fact of reality only in the material of signifying embodiment* [...] *the word has become the signifying material of inner life – of consciousness*' (MPL 9, 14). Not only must consciousness be physically and materially embodied – or 'located' – it depends for its realization, its very existence, on another material phenomenon – speech or, by extension, writing. Language in use – discourse – is the 'signifying material' of both inner *and* outer life; consciousness is not only 'embodied' in the body, it is embodied in language (discourse). In the dialogic text, specifically, meaning is *embodied* in the discourse of the character: it is 'embodied', that is, at a remove and without the need for a body.

There is more than a hint of paradox in this idea. 'Embodiment in language' would appear at first glance to be a contradiction in terms, suggesting a misconception of the properties of both terms: 'embodiment' implies the need, simply, for a material body that will act as bearer of that which is embodied in it, and language, rather than being such a bearer or vehicle, would appear to require something to be embodied in. In Voloshinov, these categories are conflated in the theorization of the sign as fundamentally material, but nonetheless 'living'; in Bakhtin, this is emphasized through a kind of literalization, which conceives of literary production in terms of the creation of living, signifying 'heroes' possessed of an open, becoming being – living subjects, embodied interlocutors for their author (and for their reader). The idea of embodiment in language thus gestures towards resolution of the opposition that has troubled Bakhtin's early work, between a precise but abstract (and therefore virtually worthless) knowledge and a purely aesthetic 'seeing'. It also renders very well the sense in which Bakhtin needs *literature*, and not 'philosophy', in order to elucidate *and* exemplify – or embody – the architectonics of self-other relations.

The somewhat disarming term Bakhtin deploys in the description of this embodiment not in the body, but in the discourse which emanates from it, the term that therefore encapsulates the living palpability of the character in literature, is *voice*: in fact, the character in Dostoevsky's novel being 'not an image, but fully-weighted discourse' is synonymous for Bakhtin with the character being 'a *pure voice*' (PDP 53) – we do not 'see' Dostoevsky's characters, we 'hear' them. Dostoevsky possesses

> the genius to hear the dialogue of his epoch or, more precisely, to hear his epoch as a great dialogue, to detect in it not just separate voices, but above all *dialogic relations* between voices, their dialogic *interaction*.
>
> (PDP 90)

And Bakhtin later describes the essence of his own project in the following simple terms: 'I hear *voices* in everything and dialogic relations between them' (TMHS 169); indeed, as Bakhtin would put it in an untranslated fragment, 'the object of the human sciences' is nothing more than '*expressive* and *speaking* being'.

It is clear, then, that 'voice' is not intended, like 'polyphony', as nothing more than a limited, 'graphic analogy', a loosely metaphorical means of expressing a broader point (PDP 22). Yet, it remains difficult to regard it entirely literally: we do not 'hear' texts, but we are, Bakhtin maintains, alive to the 'voices' that are active in them and to the 'dialogic relations' between voices. What is at stake, then, in Bakhtin's insistence on the term (an insistence that is absent in the case of 'polyphony') becomes clear if we compare its use to the well-known rejection of the 'metaphorics of presence' that Western culture has erected around the spoken word proposed by Derrida. For Derrida, orality deepens the illusion that the subject is directly present in and accessible through its performed utterance (Derrida 1981); Bakhtin, on the contrary, anticipates and resists the postmodern effacement of the subject – without the need, it would seem, for any sort of philosophical justification – by *overdetermining* presence. If 'voice' is metaphorical at all, its purpose is to *insist* on presence *above all*, to make palpable the presence in the text of autonomous subjects, who are not at the same time reducible to the intrusive and homogenizing 'presence' of the author.

Perhaps the best way of illustrating Bakhtin's conception of voice is to compare it to another significant invocation of voice – this time contemporary to Bakhtin – the Russian Formalist category of *skaz*.

RUSSIAN FORMALISM

The so-called Russian Formalists were a group of literary and linguistic scholars who coalesced around the St Petersburg-based organization *Opoiaz* (The Society for the Study of Poetic Language) in the years immediately before and after the revolutions of 1917. Iurii Tynianov (1894–1943), Viktor Shklovsky (1893–1984) and Boris Eikhenbaum (1886–1959) formed the organizational and theoretical core of the group, although their collaboration with the Moscow- and Prague-based Roman Jakobson (1896–1982), who would later exert a huge influence on the interface between literature and lin- guistics in the West, was extremely important in the years between 1918 and 1921. Early Formalist theory emphasized the *specificity* of the literary text above all else, focusing on those characteristics that make it distinct from the historical or philosophical text, and aggressively rejecting any criticism that relies on the biography or psychology of the author – or indeed any direct relationship between literature and society. This produced two main strands of theoretical work: the first focuses on the specificity of an autonomous 'poetic language', which can be counterposed to 'practical' or 'everyday' language (Jakobson, but also Lev Iakubinskii (1892–1945) and Osip Brik (1888–1945)), and the second focuses on how what had been seen as the 'content' of the literary work – themes, motifs, ideas – serves merely as the 'motivation of the device', as 'material' that is worked upon by a range of 'devices' – repetition, parallelism, retardation – a process that is once again definitive of 'literariness' (Shklovsky, Eikhenbaum). The Formalists were cri- tiqued by Bakhtin in an unpublished work of 1924 (PCMF) and again by Medvedev in 1928 (FM), but the later direction of Formal- ism, particularly the work of Iurii Tynianov, exerted its influence on both the second part of the Dostoevsky book and 'Discourse in the Novel'. *Skaz*, a key focus in the work of Eikhenbaum, is an example of a 'device' that is heavily associated with the Formalists, but which is adopted and re-inflected by Bakhtin.

Eikhenbaum's articles on Nikolai Gogol (1809–52) and Nikolai Leskov (1831–95) deal in part with a type of narration that involves emphasis of the speech characteristics of the conditional narrator, often involving colloquialism; the narrator is thus implicitly dis- tinguished from the author, who is assumed to conform to the norms of the prevailing literary style. This kind of narration, which was common in the Russian folk tale, has come to be known as '*skaz* narration', the term *skaz* evoking speech and the act of tell- ing. Eikhenbaum defines the core property of *skaz* narration as an 'orientation towards the spoken word' (Eikhenbaum 1927: 220); it is a species of narrative focalization, which is designed to create the illusion of oral narration – the presence of a distinctive 'voice' not restricted to character dialogue. Bakhtin doesn't question the value or presence of *skaz* narration; on the contrary, he insists that it is of even greater significance than Eikhenbaum suggests: '*skaz* is above all orientation towards the *speech of another*, and only then, as a consequence, towards oral speech' (PDP 191). It's not 'orality' *per se* that is paramount, nor the stylistic markers that attend it: those stylistic markers are merely surface indicators of the presence in the text of an encounter between two consciousnesses, between two 'fully-weighted' subjects of discourse – between two *voices*.

Where many of the examples given by both Eikhenbaum and Bakhtin are relatively short (Gogol's 'The Overcoat' (1842), Ivan Turgenev's (1818–83) 'Andrei Kolosov' (1844)), suggesting perhaps the difficulty of sustaining the 'illusion' of *skaz* over an extended narrative, a quite extreme, recent example of its use is James Kelman's (b. 1946) *How Late It Was, How Late* (1994), which maintains a sophisticated form of *skaz* over the length of the novel. Kelman establishes the voice of Sammy, the novel's main protagonist, at the heart of a narration which alternates between the first and third person. Sammy's dialect or non-standard language certainly reproduces the patterns of speech (Eikhenbaum), but it is also marked as the 'speech' of an other (Bakhtin); there are persistent examples in the text of the encounter between a 'first-person' and a 'third-person' voice, each of which is distinguished by the most subtle modulations of linguistic style (which might in fact remain all but indiscernible without the 'prompt' of the internal shift of perspective). Kelman not only displaces a 'standard', falsely 'objective' third-person narrative voice – the fundamental task of *skaz* – he also overcomes the conventional distance between that voice and the 'character zone' to which speech-patterned language is usually confined.

Bakhtin's conception of voice, in relation to *skaz* and in general, is therefore grounded in two mutually complementary ideas, both of which are central to his thought as a whole: first, voice implies the uniquely located, once-occurrent actuality of the human subject – it is a literal and figurative evocation of the idea of *embodiment*. Second, it prepares the idea that will crown Bakhtin's exposition of dialogism in the Dostoevsky book and form a bridge to its fullest statement in 'Discourse in the Novel' – because voice also signals the frequent presence of (at least) *two voices*. The discourse of

Dostoevsky's novels, the discourse referred to in Eikhenbaum's treatment of *skaz*, is 'discourse orientated towards the discourse of
others (double-voiced discourse)' (PDP 199). The example of *skaz*
is simply one of multitudes that demonstrate the inadequacy of
literary stylistics in dealing with what Bakhtin insists must be its
proper object, *double-voiced discourse*. *Skaz*, or parody, or stylization are undoubtedly present and active in the literary work, but
they have been treated, by the Formalists and earlier, primarily
as *compositional* forms, what the Formalists would term
'devices'. For Bakhtin, 'this problem lies deeper than the question of
superficial-compositional authorial discourse or of its superficial-
compositional removal' by various means (PDP 56); 'all these
compositional devices [...] are not in themselves capable of
destroying the monologism of the artistic world' (PDP 57). 'Form',
as understood by the Formalists, is for Bakhtin an 'exterior' or
'surface' phenomenon, which has obscured the 'deep', architectonic
form of dialogic discourse.

Bakhtin has begun with an analysis of Dostoevsky and has come,
in the process, to the projection of a new poetics, in which neither
the compositional device nor the specificity of the linguistic material
organized by that device can in themselves be definitive of discourse
type – and hence of literary form. Instead, one form of discourse
will distinguish itself from another according to the relationship of
the two (or more) voices present in it, as mediated and enabled by
the particular characteristics of the given compositional device.
Only this new poetics, attuned to the pervasiveness of double-
voiced discourse, 'an almost universal phenomenon' (PDP 40) that
is 'constructed beyond the boundaries of ordinary monologic unity'
(PDP 22), will be capable of accessing the complexities of its object,
literature. Bakhtin has begun, that is, by emphasizing that dialogism is not merely a *property* of Dostoevsky's novels, but is its
fundamental structural principle, which will determine its entire
stylistic and semantic profile; but, in a minor paradox that may tell
us something important about the practice of dialogical criticism,
before he has even managed to establish the specificity of Dostoevsky in this regard, Bakhtin comes to imply that the same is true
for *all* of modern literature, in greater or lesser degree. It is not
literature in itself that has been susceptible to 'the ideological
monologism of modern times' (PDP 88), but literary *criticism*,

which has therefore tended to obscure rather than reveal the deep dialogical roots of its object.

DIALOGIC DISCOURSE IN THE NOVEL

Written in 1934–35, while Bakhtin was in exile, 'Discourse in the Novel' opens with a statement of its intent to overcome 'the divide between abstract "formalism" and an equally abstract "ideologism"' (DN 259), not just in general terms – although this could be argued to be the achievement of Bakhtin's work taken as a whole – but specifically in terms of *literary stylistics*. The first element of this, 'formalism', is quite clear in the context of 'Discourse in the Novel'; the second element, 'ideologism', requires more explicit commentary. In the second part of his Dostoevsky book, Bakhtin has attempted to go beyond Formalism by inhabiting and re-inflecting its analytical paradigm, focusing now not on devices as such, but on how the 'dual directionality' of discourse is the prime force that moves beneath the formal-compositional surface of the literary work. Yet, the dual directionality of discourse struggles not just for recognition beneath the formal-compositional surface of the individual work, but also to free itself from the repressive stranglehold of a literary criticism in thrall to 'the ideological monologism of modern times' (PDP 88); the narrow, formalistic understanding of the literary work is in fact a specific manifestation of the general phenomenon of monologism. 'Formalism', or the tendency to conceive of literature in abstract formal terms, is itself not somehow immune to the forces of 'ideology' – it is also consistent with and representative of a particular ideological position.

In an attempt to overcome this 'divide', Bakhtin offers a classification of the types of prose discourse that goes beyond the 'superficial-compositional' (direct speech, first-person narration, dialogue, etc.), which in the Dostoevsky book looks as follows:

1. 'direct and unmediatedly intentional discourse – naming, informing, expressing, representing – calculated on the basis of unmediated understanding of its object' (PDP 186);
2. 'represented or *objectified discourse* [...] The most typical and widespread type of represented or objectified discourse is the *direct speech of characters*' (PDP 186); and

3. 'discourse orientated towards the discourse of others (double-voiced discourse) [*dvugolosoe slovo*]' (PDP 199), of which there are a number of related varieties, including the phenomena with which Bakhtin has begun his discussion, namely, stylization, parody and *skaz*.

In 'Discourse in the Novel', what has earlier been described in terms of 'dual directionality' – discourse that 'includes within itself as a necessary moment an orientation towards the discourse of another' (PDP 186) – gives way to a classification of discourse explicitly in terms of its 'dialogic orientation' (DN 279). And this classification looks somewhat different:

1. direct authorial literary-artistic narration (in all its diverse variants);
2. stylization of the various forms of oral everyday narration (*skaz*);
3. stylization of the various forms of semi-literary (written) everyday narration (the letter, the diary, etc.);
4. various forms of literary but extra-artistic authorial speech (moral, philosophical or scientific statements, oratory, ethnographic descriptions, memoranda and so forth); and
5. the stylistically individualized speech of characters.

(DN 262)

The key shift of emphasis in this new classification, aside from differences of detail, is towards a much greater focus on the influence of 'non-literary' discourse on literature and the novel; indeed, the expression 'literary but extra-artistic' in the fourth category is one of the most revealing in all of Bakhtin and will condition and drive much of his later work.

Overall, the trajectory established in the second half of the Dostoevsky book is now complete: the ability to 'hear' and artistically organize dialogic discourse is no longer emphasized as a rare (although not unique) capability of Dostoevsky as a novelist; Dostoevsky's novels are supplanted as object of analysis and vehicle of explication by the novel *as such* (although Bakhtin will focus to a great extent on the comic novel). Further, in the very act of occupying centre stage, the novel is itself subjected to a second-level questioning, which is in some ways analogous to what has happened to Dostoevsky. It becomes clear in 'Discourse in the Novel' that what Bakhtin intends by 'Novel' is not restricted to the novels of conventional literary history, but is almost surreptitiously extended to signify not a literary genre or mode, but a particular way of conceiving of language. This is consistent with the Dostoevsky book's contention that dialogical relationships 'are an almost universal phenomenon, permeating all human speech and all relationships and manifestations of human life' (PDP 40), which is now restated as follows:

> The dialogic orientation of discourse is of course a property of all discourse [...] [it] is present to a greater or lesser degree in all areas of the life of discourse.
>
> (DN 279, 284)

The implications of this shift – the sense in which the novel (never mind Dostoevsky) is not the unique location of any particular discourse 'type', but merely the genre in which dialogic discourse, a 'universal phenomenon', can best be apprehended in all its 'complexity and depth' (DN 278) – will be an important focus of later chapters.

Finally, and most importantly, 'Discourse in the Novel' expands Bakhtin's earlier, almost fleeting discussion of the 'dual directionality' of discourse, its 'double-voiced' nature, into a full-blown statement of the fundamental mechanics of dialogism – which Bakhtin now calls 'internal dialogism' in order to distinguish it from dialogue as a purely (surface) formal phenomenon. 'Internal' dialogism – or, simply, dialogism – possesses two closely related aspects or phases, which are in practical terms 'almost indistinguishable during stylistic analysis' (DN 283). The first of these relates to the way in which the 'living word' – the utterance, discourse, as opposed to the abstract word as conceived by linguistics – relates to or encounters its own object:

> Between the word and its object, between the word and the speaking subject, there exists an elastic environment of other, alien words about the same object [...] any concrete word (utterance) finds the object towards which it is directed always and already qualified, as it were,

disputed, evaluated, enveloped by an obscuring mist, or, on the contrary, by the light of other words already spoken about it. It is caught up in and penetrated by common thoughts and points of view, other evaluations and accents. The word directed towards its object enters this dialogically agitated and tension-filled environment of other words, evaluations and accents, weaves itself into their complex inter-relations, merges with some, recoils from or intersects with others; and all of this may fundamentally form the word, may leave deposits in all its semantic layers, complexify what it expresses and influence its entire stylistic profile.

(DN 276)

The sense in which the dialogic orientation of discourse is not a contingent property of one or other site of language use – the novel, for example – is complete in Bakhtin's summation that

the word is born in dialogue as a living rejoinder within it; the word is shaped in dialogic interaction with an alien word that is already in the object. *A word forms a concept of its object in a dialogic way*.

(DN 279, my emphasis)

Dialogism is the hallmark of all concrete language use; concepts are inherently dialogic – all meaning is dialogic.

The second aspect of dialogism concerns not the word's relation to its object, but, as we may have come to expect from the model of self-other relations we have repeatedly encountered throughout Bakhtin's work, the speaking subject's relation to an *anticipated response*:

[the word] encounters an alien word not only in the object itself; every word is directed towards an answer and cannot escape the profound influence of the answering word that it anticipates. [...] [it] is directly, blatantly oriented towards a future answer-word; it provokes an answer, anticipates it and structures itself in the answer's direction.

(DN 280)

Bakhtin is even prepared to argue that 'to some extent, primacy belongs to the response [...] Understanding comes to fruition only in the response' (DN 282):

> The speaker breaks through the alien conceptual horizon of the listener, constructs his own utterance on alien territory, against the listener's apperceptive background.
>
> (DN 282)

In both these senses, in relation to its object, which is surrounded on all sides by words already spoken about it, and in relation to the anticipated response of a 'listener' (or reader, or other character), 'the word lives [...] on the boundary between its own context and another, alien context' (DN 284). No human being since the mythical Adam has opened their mouth without producing dialogic discourse; no writer, however much they may strive to suppress the dialogic, can achieve the purely monologic; what Bakhtin calls 'the novel' is merely the location at which the 'kinds and degrees of otherness', the 'various forms and degrees of dialogic orientation in discourse' (DN 275–6) are at their most visible and accessible. Yet, the cause or guarantor of this capacity of the novel (as a literary genre) is not dialogism in itself – a universal phenomenon – but another key Bakhtinian concept, *heteroglossia*. Heteroglossia will allow Bakhtin to elucidate dialogism as a truly universal, *social* phenomenon, beyond (but always encompassing) the immediate frame of self-other interactions.

SUMMARY

The Dostoevsky book develops Bakhtin's model of self-other relations and its attendant concepts – eventness, answerability, embodiment, outsideness and unfinalizability – into an explicit theory of the dialogic expounded on literary material. 'Discourse in the Novel' further develops this model in the light of Voloshinov's and Bakhtin's conception of language (discourse) in order to fully realize what is only implicit in the Dostoevsky book – the *limitlessness* of the dialogic. Dialogism is more than a literary or a purely interpersonal phenomenon: it describes the condition of all verbal interaction and therefore of all conceptual, social and ideological activity. Understanding is dialogic in two senses: first, because the relationship between language and its object is dialogic, overlain with previous evaluations, with other words that have been used in relation to the object; and second, because the uttered word is always and everywhere uttered in anticipation of a response (even when it is apparently uttered in isolation). Both aspects combine seamlessly to define the 'entire stylistic profile' of what is said or written; but, more importantly, that 'stylistic profile' opens out onto and reveals the (social, ideological) situation of the utterance, in literature and beyond it – it is a stylistics of 'living language'. Experience is dialogic; the world itself is, in a sense, dialogic because no encounter with it, however determined its subject(s) may be to 'monologize', can actually take place without exposure to the dialogizing effect of the language of others, either as a 'dialogizing background' for the encounter with an object, or as an actually or implicitly anticipated response. Dialogism is the global concept towards which all elements of Bakhtin's thought gravitate.

7

HETEROGLOSSIA AND THE NOVEL

One of the central problems thematized in the previous chapter – and indeed in Bakhtin's work from the very beginning – is the question of where 'literature' begins and ends, of how and where it is contiguous with other forms of writing, and of how it relates, on a different level, to the 'life world' it evokes (and always remains part of). Late in life, Bakhtin complained to one of the younger scholars who had participated in his rediscovery that his Dostoevsky book remained locked in 'the immanent circle of literary studies', adding with apparent regret that 'there must be a way out to other worlds'. This chapter will explore, in continuation of our brief description of how 'Discourse in the Novel' crowns the concept of dialogism, the ways in which that essay marks Bakhtin's final and profound transgression of any imagined boundary between literature and 'other worlds'. In 'Discourse in the Novel' and 'The Prehistory of Novelistic Discourse', and without ever denying the importance of the literary text, Bakhtin breaks free from any perceived restriction of 'immanent' or enclosed, self-sufficient literary study and places his model of self-other relations firmly and explicitly in the context of other worlds – in the context, in fact, of the world in its entirety.

This break is achieved through the introduction of two key, mutually related ideas: *polyglossia* and *heteroglossia*. Polyglossia – literally, 'multi-languagedness' – refers to the mutual inter-animation of 'national' languages and insists that no language is or ever has been entirely self-sufficient, insulated from the influence of other languages. Heteroglossia – a less felicitous translation, which essentially refers to 'diversity of speech' – is Bakhtin's way of describing the *internal* condition of any language, its variation and stratification, produced as individual speakers and social groups interact with and against an abstract 'standard' language. These concepts also underpin Bakhtin's mature theory of the novel, as well as what he calls *novelization*, the process by which the novel form (specifically as he conceives it) influences the stylistic profile of other literary forms and of language beyond literature – or, in other words, how the novel itself is always and definitively in the process of breaking out to other worlds.

POLYGLOSSIA

Bakhtin's remarks on polyglossia are illustrative of the radically speculative style that marks much of his work from the 1930s and for which he has been admired and criticized in equal measure. It is also characteristic that he approaches polyglossia from what is at first glance an unlikely direction: reaching back into the 'lengthy history [of] novelistic discourse' (PND 50), which predates the emergence of the modern European novel by millennia, he identifies the persistence of various forms of 'parodic-travestying literature', neglected by literary history, which confront and problematize the 'direct word'. The function of this kind of literature is, quite literally, to laugh at the pretensions of any discourse that presents itself as authoritative, that purports to be entirely and one-dimensionally adequate to its object. These forms include the satyr play that typically followed the three acts of a Greek tragedy, the epic poet Homer's self-parody 'War between the Mice and the Frogs' and, later, medieval parodies of Scripture. Bakhtin will much later, in the revised version of his book on Dostoevsky, identify the extended prose narratives of Mennippean satire as a highly developed example of parodic-travestying literature, emphasizing its role in the 'prehistory' of the modern novel. Such parodic-travestying literature 'rips the word away from its object, disunifies the two'; it exposes monologic discourse as 'one-sided, bounded, incapable of exhausting its object' (PND 55):

> Parodic-travestying literature introduces the permanent corrective of laughter, of a critique of the one-sided seriousness of the lofty direct word.
>
> (PND 55)

This does not, of course, simply reflect a preference for the comic genres on Bakhtin's part, a taste for the low or the rebellious. In fact, the persistence and occasional proliferation of parodic-travestying literature is a symptom of higher-level changes in the culture in which they appear, changes which, as we will presently see, are related to changes beyond the confines of a given 'national' literature.

The 'linguistic consciousness' of the parodic-travestying point of view, in ripping the word away from its object, positions itself outside the monologic discourse it parodies. Parodic-travestying forms

> liberated the object from the power of language in which it had become entangled as if in a net; they destroyed the homogenizing power of myth over language; they freed consciousness from the power of the direct word, destroyed the thick walls that had imprisoned consciousness within its own discourse, within its own language.
>
> (PND 60)

Yet, these 'parodic antibodies' (N70 133) do not 'act alone', as it were, entirely insulated within a given literature or culture; a rag-tag collection of parodic forms – 'homeless', as Bakhtin describes them (PND 59) – could not bring about the revolution in linguistic consciousness that he has in mind all by themselves. The effect produced by parodic-travestying literature in distancing language from reality becomes clearly perceptible only in those periods when another critical light is shone on the fiction of language as a closed, self-sufficient system – the light of *another* national language. Polyglossia (multi-languagedness) demonstrates, from 'outside' as it were, that a given national language is not the *only* language, that it has developed – and continues to develop – under the influence of other cultural and linguistic forms; the parodic-travestying forms replicate this challenge to monoglot and monologic autonomy from 'within'.

As a result of the interplay between intrinsic and extrinsic forces, acting at once within and from outside a given culture, a fundamental distance, the distance of the double-voiced, is opened up between language and reality. Just as the individual subject requires *another* subject, located in a relation of outsideness, in order to become what he or she is, so too, on a global level, do languages and cultures fully acquire self-consciousness under the gaze of another language and culture. Outsideness is essential for the exposure of the pretensions of language itself, and polyglossia is the initiator and condition of possibility of this higher-level outsideness:

> Language is transformed from the absolute dogma it had been within the narrow framework of a sealed-off and impermeable monoglossia into a working hypothesis for comprehending and expressing reality.
>
> (PND 61)

In certain periods, a given society might remain 'isolated and culturally deaf' (EN 11), locked inside its own 'national myth' (PND 65), and thus more or less able to sustain the fiction of its own language as unitary and self-sufficient; in other periods, that society may be exposed directly to the linguistic and cultural influence of another society, forcing its language to renounce the myth of its own atemporal, ahistorical unitary self-sufficiency and to be objectified in comparison to another language. The paradigmatic example for Bakhtin is the disintegration of the ancient Greek 'national myth' and the transition to the bilingual or hybrid literary consciousness of the Roman Empire; the Latin writings of the Romans were conditioned by the *fact* of their Greek predecessors, their necessary awareness of 'other-languagedness'. The literary consciousness of the Roman Empire was *already and definitively hybrid*, and this hybridity is deepened and complexified in the encounter(s) between that literary consciousness and other, non-Latin-speaking peoples of the Empire. These are the conditions in which parodic-travestying forms can proliferate – echoing, as it were, the large-scale unmasking of language as profoundly double-voiced, polyglot and diverse (as opposed to monologic, monoglot and unitary). This can only happen, Bakhtin argues, under the condition of thoroughgoing polyglossia. Only polyglossia fully frees consciousness from the tyranny of its own language and its own myth of language. [...] Where languages and cultures inter-animated each other, language became something entirely different, its very nature changed: in place of a single, unitary, sealed-off Ptolemaic world of language, there appeared the open Galilean world of many languages, mutually animating each other.

(PND 61, 65)[1]

The parodic-travestying forms to which Bakhtin refers are thus harbingers of change on a far grander scale: they are both symptoms and proof of the fact that language itself has been 'transformed', that its 'very nature' has changed, and that subsequent attempts to assert its unitary, monological and monoglot nature – such as persisted and intensified from the eighteenth century through to the period in which Bakhtin was writing – are merely attempts to maintain a fiction. These forms also represent the 'prehistory' of the novel: unable to correspond to the literary system of the closed, monoglot world, with its dominant and 'finalized' genres of epic, lyric and drama, such parodic-travestying forms will eventually find a 'home' in the novel. Polyglossia, which helps make the presence of such forms more clearly perceptible as it transforms 'linguistic consciousness' at a global level, is therefore an essential precondition for the emergence of the novel.

HETEROGLOSSIA

The parodic-travestying forms through which Bakhtin has approached polyglossia are also, and perhaps more congruously, the means by which he approaches the question of the *internal* stratification of language and the concept of heteroglossia. Satyr plays and scriptural parodies cannot fit into a 'high and straightforward genre' (i.e. epic, lyric, drama) because they are too '*contradictory*' and, revealingly, too '*heteroglot*' (PND 55). In fact, polyglossia is in Bakhtin's scheme inseparable from

the problem of heteroglossia within a language, that is, the problem of internal differentiation, the stratification characteristic of any national language.

(PND 67)

Elsewhere, he speaks of 'external and internal polyglossia' (EN 12), and this is a good way of thinking about heteroglossia: as the internal complement, acting within a language, to the process of inter-animation between languages. Just as polyglossia lays bare the fiction of any national language as unitary from without, heteroglossia continues and intensifies this process from within. Polyglossia creates the conditions in which the fact of heteroglossia becomes perceptible. The two are mutually complementary, combining to 'change' language and our perception of it forever:

> Two myths perish simultaneously: the myth of a language that presumes to be the only language; and the myth of a language that presumes to be completely unified.
>
> (PND 68)

Where Bakhtin has gone no further than establishing polyglossia's role in exploding the myth of a unitary language and preparing a 'bilingual' (or multilingual) literary consciousness – that is, his analysis is extremely brief, given the scope and significance of its claims – he offers far greater detail on the 'mechanics' of heteroglossia. Polyglossia may be a precondition for the emergence of the novel, but heteroglossia, as we will see, will be the very *stuff* of the novel, the very definition of what, for Bakhtin, the novel is. Once again defined against Voloshinov's 'fiction' of a unitary, abstract language, heteroglossia refers to the condition of language as radically *stratified* into

> social dialects, characteristic group behaviour, professional jargons, generic languages, languages of generations and age groups, tendentious languages, languages of the authorities, of various circles and of passing fashions, languages that serve the specific sociopolitical purposes of the day, even of the hour (each day has its own slogan, its own vocabulary, its own emphases) – this internal stratification [is] present in every moment of its historical existence.
>
> (DN 263)

Language is therefore necessarily 'ideologically saturated' (DN 271), suffused with the views, opinions and conceptual horizons of those who make up the various social, professional and generational groupings. Language as a 'system of abstract grammatical categories' is a *theoretical construct*, a 'theoretical expression of the historical processes of linguistic unification and centralization, an expression of the *centripetal* forces of language' (DN 270, my emphasis). Yet, these forces, which have all but monopolized the attention of various schools of linguistics and philosophy of language, act within a largely unacknowledged but no less actual *heteroglossia*:

> The centripetal forces of the life of language embodied in a 'unitary language' operate in the midst of the reality of heteroglossia. At every given moment in its becoming, language is stratified not only into linguistic dialects [...], but also – and for us this is the essential point – into socio-ideological languages: the languages of social groups, 'professional' and 'generic' languages, the languages of different generations, etc. From this point of view, the literary language is itself just one of these languages of heteroglossia, and is in its turn stratified into various languages (generic, tendentious, etc). This immanent stratification and heteroglossia is not only static in the life of a language, but is dynamic, broadening and deepening as long as a language is alive and developing; alongside the centripetal forces of language there are continually active centrifugal forces: alongside verbal ideological centralization and unification there is an uninterrupted process of decentralization and separation.

> (DN 271–2)

Heteroglossia is the underlying condition of language, the 'reality' against which the centralizing and centripetal forces of official culture struggle. To study language or literature within the frame of reference of the unitary and centralizing is, for Bakhtin, to misunderstand the fundamental condition of both from the very outset.

Where, however, does the individual speaker stand amidst these forces? The danger might appear that the subject of Bakhtin's self-other model, dialogically engaging with his or her other in the once-occurrent event of being, must be overwhelmed and lost in the face of forces and properties that act universally. In fact, heteroglossia is the idea that ultimately allows Bakhtin to connect the immediate particularity of interpersonal relations to higher-level social interaction:

> Every concrete utterance of a speaking subject is a point susceptible to both centripetal and centrifugal forces. The processes of centralization

and decentralization, of unification and separation, intersect in the concrete utterance, which satisfies the demands of its 'own' language as an individualized embodiment of a speech act, but which also satisfies the demands of heteroglossia, in which it is an active participant. And this active participation of every utterance in living heteroglossia determines the linguistic style and profile of that utterance to no less a degree than its belonging to the normative-centralizing system of a unitary language.

(DN 272)

The dialogic construction of meaning is not a phenomenon restricted to the immediate encounter between subject and (listening and responding) subject in the co-event of their being; that encounter, through the language each speaks, its imbrication in the heteroglot reality of language – 'this dialogically agitated and tension-filled environment of other words, evaluations, accents' (DN 276) – is a mediation between the centripetal and centrifugal forces active in language. Living heteroglossia is *embodied* not only in the individual speaker, but also in the eventness of the encounter with another speaker/listener. (The anticipated response of the listener, a crucial factor in the dialogism of the encounter, is also and similarly imbricated in 'other words, evaluations, accents'.) Heteroglossia, a generalized property of all language-in-use, is repeatedly *dialogized* in the moment of new utterance:

The authentic environment of an utterance, the environment in which it lives and takes shape, is dialogized heteroglossia, anonymous and social as language, but simultaneously concrete, filled with specific content and accented as an individual utterance.

(DN 272)

Dialogized heteroglossia is perhaps the most important concept in Bakhtin's thought as a whole, connecting as it does the life, the moment – the event – of the individual subject/speaker to the generalized movement of language through different cultures and epochs. Heteroglossia once and for all lifts the concept of dialogism, present in embryonic form in Bakhtin's thought from the very beginning, out of the realm of the purely interpersonal – but without severing its essential connection with that realm. It also lifts dialogism decisively out of the realm of the 'purely literary', justifying its definition as a 'universal phenomenon, permeating all human speech and all relationships and manifestations of human life, everything that has meaning and significance' (PDP 40); as it is now restated in 'Discourse in the Novel', 'the dialogic orientation of discourse is, of course, a property of *any* discourse. It is the natural orientation of any living discourse' (DN 279). Yet Bakhtin, in a manner that poses radical questions concerning the relationship between discourse in the interpersonal, 'universal' and literary contexts, immediately re-immerses heteroglossia in the world of literature – or, more specifically, in the world of the novel.

HETEROGLOSSIA AND THE NOVEL

What, however, *is* a novel from the point of view of what Bakhtin has dismissed as 'traditional stylistics', locked in a deadening embrace with a conception of language as abstract and unitary? The answer is, without exaggeration, almost nothing: the novel eludes the grasp of traditional stylistics, which cannot 'isolate a single definite, stable characteristic of the novel' (EN 8) without immediately qualifying and thus destroying that characteristic as a generic marker. Even the banality of defining the novel as an 'extended work of prose fiction' cannot withstand the pressure of the radical variation in length the genre can apparently bear (try comparing Victor Hugo's *Les Misérables* (1862) to Albert Camus' *L'Étranger* (1942) on any meaningful formal or stylistic basis), or the fact that there are, albeit in limited quantity, novels in verse (Bakhtin is fond of involving Pushkin's novel in verse *Eugene Onegin* (1833)), or the fact that even the assumed *fictionality* of the novel becomes subject to legitimate doubt in works such as Truman Capote's *In Cold Blood* (1966) or, more recently, David Peace's *GB84* (2004).

For Bakhtin, on the contrary, and in expression of his alternative, higher-level stylistics of dialogized heteroglossia,

> the novel can be defined as a diversity of social speech types (sometimes even diversity of languages) and a diversity of individual voices, artistically organized.
>
> (DN 262)

and

> every novel is a dialogized system made up of the images of 'languages',
> styles and consciousnesses [...].
>
> (PND 49)

From the reverse perspective, as well as depending on heteroglossia
for its definition (and, for Bakhtin, its very existence), the novel
is in fact the *only* location at which all the diversity implied by
heteroglossia can in practice be observed:

> All languages of heteroglossia, whatever the principle underlying them
> and making each unique, are specific points of view on the world, forms
> for conceptualizing the world in words, specific world views, each char-
> acterized by its own objects, meaning and values. As such they all may
> be juxtaposed to one another, mutually supplement one another, contra-
> dict one another and be interrelated dialogically. As such they encounter
> one another and co-exist in the consciousness of real people – first and
> foremost, in the creative consciousness of people who write novels.
>
> (DN 291–2)

The novel may indeed be a uniquely privileged site for the apprehension of heteroglossia, but this must not obscure the sense in
which heteroglossia is primarily a *social fact*; heteroglossia
describes the fundamental condition of language (discourse),
encompassing all forms of verbal interaction, literary and otherwise. The novel is, however, uniquely receptive to heteroglossia,
which grows out of the heteroglot (and polyglot) condition of language; the novel absorbs and dialogically inter-animates the various
strata of heteroglot language, embodied in the discourse of the
author and the speech of characters, imagined as belonging to a
diverse array of 'social groups'. It makes heteroglossia perceptible: it is, to revert to terms used earlier, both a 'laboratory of
creation' and a *'powerful condenser of unspoken social evaluations'*
(DLDP 76).

This unique receptivity to heteroglossia makes the novel the only
'genre in a state of becoming' (EN 11); it is therefore, in a radical
restatement of Bakhtin's concept of unfinalizability, now at the level
of literary and social history, the only genre that 'can comprehend

the process of becoming' (EN 7) – in other words, the only genre adequate to the essential 'becomingness' of human existence, to the living flux of human experience and the discourse in which it is embodied.

The author of a novel, then, rather than simply developing plot, character or theme utilizing whichever stylistic means are available, organizes and *orchestrates*[2] the discursive strata of a heteroglot language into a multilayered complex of dialogized 'images of language', each reflecting the world view of an embodied subject. The word itself is 'shot through with the dialogized overtones' of social heteroglossia (DN 279) – a fact of the life of language, within and beyond literature – but each word, each potential utterance is further activated in the novel as it is dialogically juxtaposed to the words and potential utterances of other characters and of the author. This conception of the relationship of the author to the work and the characters in it fully realizes all the implications of the near-equivalent status he attributes to self-other and author-hero relationships from his earliest work. The hero or character is not merely represented or created by the author, but is rather 'located in a zone of potential conversation with the author, in a zone of *dialogical contact*' (PND 45); the language of the novel is not uniformly the language of the author, but often 'the image of another's language' (PND 44); just as 'the word in language is half someone else's' (DN 293), words in the novel do not pertain entirely to the linguistic consciousness of the author, who thereby cedes control of large areas of the stylistic fabric of his or her creation. In Pushkin's *Eugene Onegin* (a novel in verse), for example,

> the author is far from neutral in his relationship to [the image of another's language], argues with it, agrees with it (although with conditions), interrogates it, eavesdrops on it, but also ridicules it, parodically exaggerates it and so forth – in other words, the author is in a dialogical relationship with Onegin's language; the author is actually conversing with Onegin, and such a conversation is the fundamental constitutive element of all novelistic style [...]. The author represents [Onegin's language], carries on a conversation with it, and the conversation penetrates into the interior of this language-image and dialogizes it from within. And all essentially novelistic images share this quality: they are internally dialogized

images – of the languages, styles, world views of another (all of which are
inseparable from their concrete linguistic and stylistic embodiment).

(PND 46)

As we saw in Chapter 6 in relation to Dostoevsky – initially offered
as something quite particular and now revealed as exemplary of a
much broader phenomenon – a 'single and unified authorial consciousness' (PDP 9) is therefore a fiction. The author is of course
present in the text, but, in the act of creating the novel's characters,
he or she accords them the status of 'not only the objects of the
authorial word, but also subjects of their own signifying word'
(PDP 7), whose voices combine 'in a particular way' with 'the
authorial word and with the equally valued voices of the other
characters' (PDP 7). The language of another is therefore 'simultaneously represented and representing' in the novel (PND 45); it is
both the immediate object of authorial representation and a kind of
filter – social, discursive, conceptual – through which the world of
the novel and its events are represented. The author represents the
language of another, and this language, in turn, participates in
the representation of the world internal to the novel. The whole of
the world is bathed in the light of dialogized heteroglossia: not just
language, but objects, situations, concepts and historical events are
all effectively dialogized in the novel.

This is true also of the *literary language* of any given tradition,
which, in a parallel with the individual speaker (in life and in literature), is 'susceptible to both centripetal and centrifugal forces' (DN
272) and which itself undergoes constant change in the process:

The national literary language of a people with a highly developed art of
prose [...] is in fact an organized microcosm that reflects the macrocosm
[...] of national heteroglossia.

(DN 295)

The idea of social heteroglossia therefore facilitates a radical
update on the nature of the 'particular way' in which the other
voices present in the novel combine with 'the authorial word and
with the equally valued voices of the other characters' (PDP 7),
broadening the focus from the narrow frame of interpersonal and
intra-literary relations to the maximal frame of the totality of

social relations. Heteroglossia represents the 'globalization' of the dialogic principle through and beyond the literary.

INTERLUDE: HYBRID CONSTRUCTIONS IN DICKENS

Bakhtin calls those fragments of a novel in which another voice (or voices) dialogically interacts with the voice of the author 'stylistic hybrids' (PND 76) or 'hybrid constructions' (DN 304); not just two languages, but two *voices*, two world views, two 'live' consciousnesses are perceptible in the hybrid construction 'without any of the *formal markers*' (DN 303) that might normally accompany and indeed advertise the presence of two voices (marking it off as dialogue or reported speech, for example). Such hybrid constructions appear where particular compositional forms are utilized to introduce and organize heteroglossia in the novel – chiefly in development of the idea of the periodic proliferation of parodic-travestying literature, what Bakhtin calls 'parodic stylization' (DN 301); and this Bakhtin exemplifies mainly through 'the English comic novel' and, in particular, *Little Dorrit* (1857) by Charles Dickens (1812–70). For example, Mr Merdle is described by Dickens in book 2, ch. 12 as follows:

> *O, what a wonderful man this Merdle, what a great man, what a master man, how blessedly and enviably endowed* – in one word, what a rich man!

Where conventional analysis might simply identify light comic irony in the narrator's belated commentary on his *own* initial statement, Bakhtin insists on the presence of two voices, which are not compositionally marked in any way in the original text (the first of which, not 'belonging' to the author or narrator, is marked here in italics); the italicized portion is a ventriloquized rendering of the opinion of 'society', and the final statement a comment on it from the point of view of the narrator. Similarly, even the apparently unremarkable observation that 'Mr Tite Barnacle was a buttoned-up man, and *consequently* a weighty one' (also book 2, ch. 12), provokes the observation that, judged by purely formal markers,

> the logic motivating the sentence appears to belong to the author [or narrator] [...]; but in actual fact the motivation lies within the subjective belief system of his characters, or of general opinion.
>
> (DN 305)

It is not the author or narrator who judges 'weightiness' to correlate to the quality of being 'buttoned-up'; the author/narrator observes this association to be part of the implied world view of the environment in which Barnacle and other characters in the novel exist.

The second of these brief examples also demonstrates that, while parodic stylization is one of the key compositional means by which heteroglossia enters the novel, parodic intention is far from being an absolute prerequisite for the double-voiced. As any reader of Dickens will recognize, his prose is saturated with such hybrid constructions, and not only in its comic passages. In *Bleak House* (1853), for example, where Dickens experiments with two separate narrators (one omniscient, the other the intra-diegetic Esther Summerson, Dickens' only feminine narrator), the discursive profiles of both repeatedly fragment in ways that might, at a surface level, indicate lack of stylistic control; at the level of dialogic analysis, however, which seeks to establish the heteroglot elements that dialogically interact and inter-animate beneath the formal and stylistic 'surface', such fragmentation becomes a strength – evidence, in fact – of the novel's sensitivity to the heteroglot macrocosm from which its voices and world views are hewn. Book 5, ch. 14, for example, is narrated from Esther's point of view, but its multiplicity of 'voice' is immediately signalled by its title, 'Deportment', which bears the ironic signature of the omniscient narrative voice – an irony that is intensified with every repetition of the word as the chapter progresses. Caddy Jellyby first describes Prince Turveydrop's father to Esther and Ada as follows:

> 'Very gentlemanly, indeed', said Caddy. '*He is celebrated, almost everywhere, for his deportment*'.
>
> 'Does he teach?' asked Ada.
>
> 'No, he don't teach anything in particular', replied Caddy. '*But his deportment is beautiful*'.

The opening of each of Caddy's remarks is given in her 'own' discourse ('don't teach'), but is on each occasion capped by her repetition of received opinion; her speech is infected by the discourse not of Esther, who is party to and narrates the event, but of the nominally absent omniscient narrator, who is closest to the consciousness and discourse of Dickens himself. Similarly, when Caddy goes on to describe Prince Turveydrop himself:

> *'Young Mr Turveydrop's name is Prince*; I wish it wasn't, because it sounds like a dog, *but of course he didn't christen himself'*.

The first italicized segment belongs to the discourse of Esther, as if she were recounting it direct to the reader; the following expression of regret is that of both Esther and Caddy; and the final italicized segment is once again the ironized discourse of the nominally absent omniscient narrator ('Dickens'). The overall effect is of a conversation between Caddy and an empathetic Esther overheard and 'framed' for comic effect by a (nominally absent) authorial voice. Only Caddy 'speaks', but the discourse is heteroglot, socially differentiated – its stylistic profile reveals the architectonics of the event of the encounter of no less than three consciousnesses.

Such stylistic hybrids are present throughout Dickens, and it's Bakhtin's contention that they are in fact present, in whatever degree, in any novelistic prose. When we turn to twentieth-century novels in which the dramatization and exposure of socially, ethnically and gender-determined relationships is the explicit goal, however, the range and profile of the stylistic hybrids we might identify in a writer such as Dickens begin to appear either limited or, conversely, extremely refined and subtle. The ostensible distance between Caddy Jellyby and Esther Summerson, for example, taken as 'point[s] susceptible to both centripetal and centrifugal forces', each of whom brings her own socially, generationally and professionally marked language to the dialogue, is relatively short. Were we to substitute the encounter between Spud Murphy and his interrogators at a job interview he has been compelled to attend by the Unemployment Benefit Office in Irvine Welsh's (b. 1958) *Trainspotting* (1993), for example, the range of heteroglot languages in play becomes hugely extended, the matrix of social forces becomes more complex; more significantly, the *intentionality* of the hybrid constructions becomes more profound, their commentary and judgement on the events and context of the novel more explicit. It is worth noting, however, that this is also true in the ostensibly near monolingual world of Kelman's *How Late It Was, How Late*, in which the 'elements' of the hybrid constructions are drawn from a 'single' dialect; they remain, however, hybrid constructions because two voices and two consciousnesses are present in them – however similar those two voices might seem.

Intentional stylistic hybrids allow the novel to extrapolate from the 'local', interpersonal event to broader societal and epochal generalizations, but without losing the force of immediacy traditionally associated with fictional characterization reconceived in the specifically Bakhtinian terms of the architectonics of the event. The novel, whether in the macrocosmic domains of postcoloniality or class or gender relations, or the microcosmic domain of interpersonal relations, is a machine for the dialogization of socially heteroglot languages, a unique 'common plane' upon which, as we have seen, the languages of heteroglossia confront and inter-animate one another.

NOVELIZATION

This unique capacity of the novel has clear and significant implications for all other literary forms and genres, which might be approached by returning to a question already implied: if language is fundamentally heteroglot, and dialogism a 'universal phenomenon, permeating all human speech and all relationships and manifestations of human life, everything that has meaning and significance' (PDP 40), why is Bakhtin so insistent in his claim that poetry, rather than being merely less congenial or receptive, is in fact actively *resistant* to dialogized heteroglossia? The answer to this question can be found in the *obverse* of Bakhtin's contention that the dialogic dynamism of the novel, 'the only genre younger than writing and the book' (EN 3), is brought into being through the activation of a bilingual or multilingual literary consciousness associated with polyglossia and heteroglossia. Poetry, on the contrary, like epic (whether in verse or not), had already been accorded a canonical position as the predominant literary mode of an *abstractly conceived unitary language*. 'The concept of poetic discourse, which had been at the heart of all concepts of style' is one historical 'expression of the centripetal forces of language' (DN 270), in fact the dominant literary expression of those forces, which draws all other forms of literary expression into its orbit (hence the tendency of 'organic stylistics' to misunderstand the novel). The novel, the vehicle and product of dialogized heteroglossia, has been viewed as a defective 'poetic' genre by centuries of criticism that is itself an expression of 'the ideological monologism of modern times' (PDP 88), the vehicle and product of the concept of a unitary language. A critical viewpoint that seeks to establish the 'higher stylistics' of dialogized heteroglossia must therefore, from the reverse perspective, expose poetry as a defective 'novelistic' genre. Poetic discourse, Bakhtin argues, cannot be the primary vehicle of 'multi-languaged consciousness' and 'double-voiced discourse' because it was formed in the epoch of the predominance of their opposites, the epoch of the monoglot, the unitary and the centralizing.

Latter-day readers of Bakhtin may reasonably object not only that he himself offers repeated exemplification on poetic material – Dante, Pushkin, Rilke – but, moreover, that the direction of modern poetry since Bakhtin – from Frank O'Hara (1926–66) to Benjamin Zephaniah (b. 1958) – has resoundingly disproved any implication of the dialogic and heteroglot limitations of poetry due to its *genesis* in monoglossia. Bakhtin's disarming response is that this, simply, is entirely consistent with his theory because poetry, in the epoch of the rise and eventual domination of the novel, has gradually but decisively become *novelized*:

> In many respects the novel has anticipated, and continues to anticipate, the future development of literature as a whole. In the process of becoming the dominant genre, the novel facilitates the renovation of all other genres, it infects them with its spirit of becoming and unfinalizability. It draws them ineluctably into its orbit precisely because this orbit coincides with the basic direction of the development of literature as a whole.
>
> (EN 7)

Poetry has sought to shut out the light of dialogized heteroglossia and to conceive of objects, situations, concepts and historical events in its own, unitary language; but it begins to 'sound [...] in new ways' as the novel gradually overcomes the monologic past. Even the poet, once 'utterly immersed in [his own language] as a pure and direct expression of his own intention' (DN 285), operates 'in the midst of the reality of heteroglossia' (DN 271).

This is perhaps the most extreme example, in the specifically literary context, of Bakhtin's repeated insistence on the prevalence of architectonic form over 'surface, compositional form': in the case of language generally, the architectonic form of the utterance, embodying all the elements of the concrete speech situation, is preferred to the purely abstract 'surface' form of the sentence; in literature, architectonic form embodies the matrix of dialogized heteroglot elements present in the work and is preferred to 'surface' formal indicators (rhythm, metre, etc.). Bakhtin, returning to parody as his favoured form for the revelation of underlying discursive relations, is even prepared to argue that 'parodied genres do not belong to the genres they parody; that is, a parodic poem is not a poem at all' (PND 59). Elsewhere, dismissing the majority of 'historians of literature' at a stroke, Bakhtin insists that what such historians usually call a 'romantic poem' is in fact a 'novelized poem' (EN 7); genre itself is not a question of surface, compositional form, but of the extent to which any form or mode has been novelized – has become receptive to or determined by dialogized heteroglossia.

SUMMARY

Heteroglossia describes the internal stratification of a national language into a series of 'social dialects', which are ideologically saturated with the world views of their speakers; it is the internal correlative of *polyglossia*, which describes the mutual inter-animation of national languages, the moment at which language in general is distanced from itself, and from which its essentially double-voiced nature becomes undeniable – actively constitutive of a new form of linguistic consciousness. Heteroglossia is the concept that explicitly extends Bakhtin's core model of self-other relations beyond the localized domain of interpersonal relations; it also extends the range of Bakhtin's theory of literary language beyond the limits of 'literature', conventionally conceived. The novel emerges not only as the literary genre that is uniquely and maximally receptive to social heteroglossia – a *social* as opposed to a literary fact – but in fact as the pre-eminent location at which the many languages of heteroglossia can be observed in their mutual inter-animation. The novel facilitates the dialogic encounter of 'images of language', *dialogized heteroglossia*, which becomes the very definition of the novel. Each individual speaker, every 'concrete utterance' – in the novel and, by implication, in social life – is a point susceptible to the centripetal and centrifugal forces of language; each individual speaker – and every concrete utterance – is therefore a point at which language actively remakes itself and evolves in the process of its living use. The effects of this active, living evolution of a heteroglot language are also manifest elsewhere in the literary system, as other genres and modes become increasingly 'novelized' as heteroglossia increasingly predominates and its 'carrier', the novel itself, becomes the dominant literary genre. In the process, the boundaries between literature and social life, between literary and non-literary language become increasingly porous; literature, language and culture are dialogically alive 'on the boundary between [their] own context and another, alien context' (DN 284).

NOTES

1 Bakhtin refers to the mathematician and astronomer Ptolemy (c. 90–168 A.D.), whose model of the universe was eventually overturned by Galileo Galilei (1564–1642), one of the most significant figures in the emergence of modern science.
2 Polyphony, as we have seen in Chapter 6, is a metaphor for Bakhtin, but a suggestive one.

8

CHRONOTOPE

Chronotope, a term originating in science and mathematics, is introduced into literary and cultural study by Bakhtin in the long essay 'Forms of Time and of the Chronotope in the Novel', which was largely written in 1937–38, but published in Russian only in 1975 (and in English in 1981). The word consists simply of the Greek terms *khronos* (time) and *topos* (space), and it is defined, in a manner that is uncharacteristically forthright for Bakhtin, as 'the intrinsic connectedness of temporal and spatial relationships that are artistically expressed in literature' (FTC 84). Somewhat similar to Bakhtin's earlier disclaimer regarding the metaphorical nature of the term 'polyphony' – a 'graphic analogy, nothing more' (PDP 22) – chronotope is borrowed for literary criticism 'almost as a metaphor (almost, but not entirely)' (FTC 84); there is, however, a great deal in this 'not entirely', as chronotope proves to be a more self-contained and self-sufficient category than polyphony (which, as we have seen, is little more than a convenient staging post between Bakhtin's original model of self-other relations and its mature expression in the concept of dialogism). Chronotope is a powerful and adaptable framing device for literary analysis, which, Bakhtin argues, also has 'an intrinsic generic significance. It can even be said that it is precisely the chronotope that defines genre and generic distinctions' (FTC 84–5); this chapter will therefore first approach chronotope as a specifically literary category, outlining its value in terms of narrative and genre, and then expand this analysis to consider the utility of the chronotope beyond the purely literary domain.

TIME (MOSTLY) AND SPACE

Bakhtin locates the chronotope in the Kantian insistence that space and time are 'indispensable forms of any cognition, beginning with elementary perceptions and representations' (FTC 85), but diverges in his own insistence that space and time are not 'transcendental' categories, but 'forms of the most immediate reality' (FTC 85). This is developed in a manner that vividly conjures up not only the centrality for Bakhtin of both embodiment and unfinalizability, but also the enduring presence of his model of self-other relations conceived in their eventness:

> In the literary artistic chronotope, spatial and temporal indicators are fused into one carefully thought-out, concrete whole. Time, as it were, thickens, takes on flesh, becomes artistically visible; similarly, space becomes charged and responsive to the movements of time, plot and history.
>
> (FTC 84)

The chronotope functions as the

> primary means for materializing time in space, [...] for concretizing representation, as a force giving body to the entire novel. All the novel's abstract elements – philosophical and social generalizations, ideas, analyses of cause and effect – gravitate towards the chronotope and through it take on flesh and blood.
>
> (FTC 250)

The chronotope is a way of differentiating and classifying the ways in which the image of the human subject, inseparable from but irreducible to the body that occupies space and moves through time, is represented (but not finalized) in the literary text. This classification will turn on the capability of the temporal and spatial values of any given fictional environment to facilitate the 'possession' of the eventness of being, to permit the representation of a living image, as opposed to one that might variously be described as 'abstract', 'fixed' or 'monological'. Although the chronotope is therefore clearly closely related to earlier categories and concepts in Bakhtin, it is distinctive in that it emerges at the apparent *expense* of an insistence on the primary importance of language, which has driven the key shifts in Bakhtin's thought to this point. Heteroglossia and an *explicit* focus on the dialogic now recede from the foreground of Bakhtin's thought; the chronotope represents a parallel attempt to reconceive Bakhtin's core precepts for the particular purpose of literary analysis, if not quite 'without' language, then at least in a manner that implies some form of retreat from the absolute centrality of language. Language itself now becomes an (almost) secondary phenomenon, which, as we will later see, must also be conceived chronotopically.

Time, as opposed to language, is in fact 'the primary category in the chronotope [...] in literature' (FTC 85); the chronotope is a way of 'seeing' time in the physical and spatial world. Where literature, from the Greek 'novel' to the realist novel of the nineteenth century, has been adept at representing the (physical) 'image of man', such literatures, themselves divergent in place and time, can be distinguished in terms of the particular 'form of time' which organizes and conditions their representation of the physical world and the characters moving through it. Just as time is 'visible' in the represented image, so too, within different chronotopes, are people and places represented as susceptible to the movement of time (and history). Chronotopes are ways of describing the narrative frame of a particular work – and perhaps of a particular genre or epoch – in unified temporal and spatial terms, and hence of understanding the significance of everything that moves or is represented within that frame. In certain literatures, in certain chronotopes, and in relation to certain characters and situations, there may be – to put it crudely – more or less of such 'movement'. It is Bakhtin's task in 'Forms of Time and of the Chronotope in the Novel' to present a provisional typology of the different 'novelistic chronotopes' that have evolved through the history of European literature, beginning with the Greek novel and focusing largely on François Rabelais (c. 1494–1553) on the way to the modern period. We will select particular elements of Bakhtin's typology in order to give a practical description of chronotopes in action and an exemplification of their use and value in literary analysis, also making reference where appropriate to two works in which the significance of the chronotope for literary history is developed further, namely 'The *Bildungsroman* and its Significance in the History of Realism (Toward a Historical Typology of the Novel)' (1936–8) and 'Epic and Novel' (1941).

ADVENTURE-TIME AND BIOGRAPHICAL TIME ON THE ROAD TO BECOMING

Bakhtin identifies a form of time in the Greek 'novel' or 'romance' which he terms 'adventure-time', the use of which in novels such as the *Aethiopica* of Heliodorus of Emesa (c. 220–50 A.D.) 'is so perfected, so full, that in all subsequent evolution of the purely adventure novel nothing essential has been added to it down to the present day' (FTC 87). Although the action of the plot typically 'unfolds against a very broad and varied geographical background', and although the characters 'experience a most improbable number of adventures', typically in the form of the experiencing of ordeals and the overcoming of obstacles (FTC 88, 90), they emerge essentially unchanged. Time is 'not measured off in the novel and does not add up; it is simply days, nights, hours, moments' (FTC 90). This adventure-time

> lacks any natural, everyday cyclicity, which might have introduced into it a temporal order and indices on a human scale, which might have connected it to the repetitive aspects of natural and human life. [...] [The] time-sequences [of the Greek romance] are neither historical, quotidian, biographical, nor even biological or maturational. [...] In this time, nothing changes: the world remains exactly as it was, the biographical life of the heroes does not change, their feelings also remain unchanged – people do not even age.
>
> (FTC 91)

In the Roman 'novels' *The Golden Ass* of Apuleius (c. 125–80 A.D.) and the *Satyricon* of Petronius (c. 27–66 A.D.), however, adventure-time combines with what Bakhtin calls 'everyday time'; moreover, their plots are driven by the device of metamorphosis:

> Metamorphosis (transformation) is a mythological sheath for the idea of development – but one that unfolds not so much in a straight line as

spasmodically, a line with 'knots' in it [...]. On the basis of metamorphosis, a new kind of representation is created, a representation of a
whole human life in its fundamental, *critical* moments: *how a person
becomes other.*

(FTC 113, 115)

The combination of adventure-time and everyday time is not quite
yet a 'biographical time', in that it 'depicts only the exceptional,
utterly unusual moments of a person's life, moments that are very
short compared to the whole length of a human life'; but it is distinct from pure adventure-time, which 'leaves no traces': 'on the
contrary, it leaves a deep and irradicable mark' (FTC 116). It is a
property of a different, more complex chronotope than the adventure chronotope in its pure form and therefore permits a more
sophisticated representation (artistic finalization) of the human
subject in all his or her concrete, and, here at least, only *to some
extent developing* actuality. It remains, however, inadequate for
the construction of a narrative that will fulfil what is promised in
the phrase '*how a person becomes other*', that will allow the representation of 'becoming [*stanovlenie*] in the precise sense of the word'
(FTC 115).[1] It cannot yet deal with all the complexity and movement of what Bakhtin has earlier termed 'the historical actuality of
[...] being', 'actually becoming being' (TPA 2, 1).

Bakhtin's treatment of 'Ancient Biography and Autobiography'
(FTC 130–46) is designed to signal the next phase of development
of forms of time and the chronotope, a phase in which biographical
time emerges to allow a type of representation 'to new specifica-
tions, that of an individual who passes through the course of a
whole life' (FTC 130). This trajectory is perhaps clearer to the
modern reader in that part of Bakhtin's essay on the *Bildungsroman* (BSHR) – or novel of formation or upbringing – that survived
the double threat of German bombing and scarcity of cigarette
papers; indeed, the *Bildungsroman*, fundamentally defined by a
concern with how its main character 'becomes other' in the context
of a 'whole human life' (his or her own), is perhaps the clearest
example of a genre defined by its chronotope. The essay on the
Bildungsroman in fact advertises its own central concern as the
representation of 'the image of man in a *state of becoming* in
the novel' through the 'assimilation of real historical time and the

real historical person' (BSHR 19). It does not seek to distinguish chronotopes and their exemplification only in particular antique novels, but in all novelistic sub-genres classified 'according to the principle of the construction of the image of the main hero' (BSHR 10). The resultant typology is implicitly hierarchical, progressing from what Bakhtin now calls the 'travel novel', dependent on adventure-time (BSHR 10–11), through the 'novel of ordeal', to an account of the 'biographical novel's' development of an 'absolutely real' biographical time that mirrors the section on 'Ancient Biography and Autobiography' referred to above. Whereas the plot in the novel of ordeal is always focused on a deviation 'from the normal social and biographical course of life' (BSHR 14) and the tests or ordeals to which the hero is subjected 'do not become formative experience for him [*sic*], they do not change him' (BSHR 13), the plot in biographical time 'is not constructed on deviations from the normal and typical course of life, but precisely on the basic and typical aspects of any life course: birth, childhood [etc.]' (BSHR 17); 'every event is localized in the whole of this life process' (BSHR 18), and the hero is brought into real, concrete interaction with his or her environment and its temporal coordinates. Biographical time is itself limited, however, and does not permit 'any true process of becoming or development'; this is because the events of the life depicted are contained within the time frame of that life and do 'not yet know true historical time' (BSHR 18). The world beyond the life depicted is visible and does not act merely as a 'backdrop' to that life; however, the events of the novel do not affect the world beyond it.

Beyond the biographical 'novel', there are a range of novels that Bakhtin explicitly terms 'novels of becoming', of which the earliest *Bildungsroman* of the late eighteenth century is a threshold example. The chronotope of these novels is determined by their 'degree of assimilation of real historical time' (BSHR 21); the key point, however, is not that the degree of such assimilation remains limited even in the *Bildungsroman* – its 'world, as an experience and as a school, remained the same, fundamentally immobile and ready-made, given' (BSHR 23) – but that 'the assimilation of real historical time' becomes the primary objective of the novel, a proxy for the extent to which this or that type of novel is adequate to the representation of the world – and the human being in it – in the fullness of their emergence. Bakhtin is unashamedly searching for a type of novel in which, finally,

> the becoming of a person is accomplished in real historical time, with all its necessity and fullness, with its future and its profound chronotopicity.
>
> (BSHR 23)

Dickens' *David Copperfield* (1850) is identified as a further incremental advance on the *Bildungsroman* as such, still dominated by biographical time, but in which nonetheless 'the emergence of man's life destiny fuses with the emergence of man himself' (BSHR 22). It is Goethe's *Wilhelm Meister* (1795–6), however, that most completely fulfils the novel's role as the means of assimilation of real historical time, taking the novel of emergence to a further stage of its development. Here, the world is no longer 'an immobile orientation point for developing man' (BSHR 23). The emergence of the character, his or her development, his or her becoming other,

> is no longer man's own private affair. He emerges *along with the world* and he reflects the historical emergence of the world itself. He is no longer within an epoch, but on the border between two epochs, at the transition point from one to another [...] It is as though the very foundations of the world are changing, and man must change along with them.
>
> (BSHR 23–4)

These are not the only chronotopes identified by Bakhtin as being significant for the development of Western literature and for the novel in particular. He devotes considerable attention to the *idyllic chronotope*, which is marked by a 'folkloric time' and the close relation of events to a 'little spatial world [...] limited and sufficient unto itself' (FTC 225; 224–36); he devotes even more attention to the exceptional, but for Bakhtin extremely important, case of the *Rabelaisian chronotope*, which is in some ways related to the idyllic chronotope, but which has an expanded definition as 'the completely unrestricted, universal chronotope of human life' (FTC 242; 167–206) – we might even be tempted to rename this the *utopian chronotope* were it not for the terminological contradictions implied by such a name (*utopia* – lit. 'no place'). He also, in a series of remarkable passages appended to the chronotope essay in

1973 prior to its publication (to which we will have cause to return), enumerates a series of 'minor' chronotopes that derive from and supplement the major categories he has built around adventure-time, biographical time and, finally, emergence and real historical time. These include the *chronotope of the road*, a variant of the *chronotope of encounter*, in which 'time, as it were, fuses together with space and flows in it (forming the road); [...] its fundamental pivot is the flow of time' (FTC 243–4); the *chronotope of the castle*, characteristic of the Gothic novel and significant also for the development of the historical novel (FTC 245–6); the *chronotope of the provincial town*, a variation of the idyllic chronotope, in which space is strictly delimited and time is a blend of the cyclical and the everyday (FTC 247–8); and the *chronotope of the threshold*, which emphasizes crisis and dislocation in the course of events and which is characterized by sudden or instantaneous action (FTC 248). These individual chronotopes are not necessarily marked by a single form of time, but evolve through the incorporation of different and sometimes even potentially contradictory forms, as we have seen at the outset in the example of *The Golden Ass* of Apuleius' merging of adventure-time and everyday time.

Similarly, if we return to the point in Bakhtin's analysis where the so-called 'realist' novel of the nineteenth century is poised to emerge and 'complete' the process of maximizing 'the degree of assimilation of real historical time', it is important to emphasize that novels are not necessarily – or even often – determined by the influence of a single chronotope. Different novels will be defined by aspects of more than one chronotope, each influencing the whole in differing degrees. Each individual novel acts as a 'carrier' for chronotopes that have passed down through literary history, and, in fact, the ways in which those chronotopes are organized in the novel will define the way its narrative is shaped. As Bakhtin writes:

> Within the limits of a single work and within the total literary output of a single author we may notice a number of different chronotopes and complex interactions among them, specific to the given work or author; it is common moreover for one of these chronotopes to envelop or dominate the others [...]. Chronotopes are mutually inclusive,

> they co-exist, they may be interwoven with, replace or oppose one
> another, contradict one another or find themselves in ever more complex
> interrelationships.
>
> (FTC 252)

The mode of this coexistence will determine the narrative and stylistic profile of a given work more, say, than its relationship to such
literary categories as 'realism' or 'symbolism'.

A concrete example might serve to illuminate this important
point. Charlotte Brontë's *Jane Eyre* (1847) might be said to be
framed principally by biographical time and to conform in large
part to the profile of the *Bildungsroman* (particularly in its earlier
chapters at Gateshead and Lowood). Yet this dominant frame is
complicated by the presence in the novel of elements of the Gothic
and the 'chronotope of the castle', which frames the events at
Thornfield and casts the romantic narrative involving Jane and
Rochester in a light quite different to that of, for example, the
idyllic chronotope, in which the resolution of the central romantic
plot is never in doubt (the demands of a cyclical, folkloric time).
Yet, the events at Thornfield are also concentrically contained by
what we might call a *colonial chronotope*, which in the person of
Bertha Mason fuses with the Gothic to produce uniquely powerful
narrative contradictions. The entire narrative is structured by the
interrelationships of the novel's chronotopes. Moreover, the idyllic
chronotope is not absent from the novel, and the drama of the
recovery or renunciation of the idyll, which Bakhtin identifies as
being crucial for the development of the novel, is played out –
fused to Jane's spiritual (and social) quest – in her salvation at
Marsh End and, finally, in the restoration of the idyll – and the
apparent resolution of the narrative's contradictions – at Ferndean.
The idyllic chronotope, fused to the biographical growth implied
by the *Bildungsroman*, has eventually driven the Gothic (the
chronotope of the castle is destroyed with the significantly foretold
destruction of Thornfield Hall) and the colonial chronotopes to the
invisible margins of the narrative. In a parallel with Bakhtin's
summation of Goethe's *Wilhelm Meister*, 'the process of a
[woman's!] re-education is interwoven with the process of society's
breakdown and reconstruction, that is, with historical process'
(FTC 234). The extent to which 'society's breakdown and

reconstruction' is implied or reflected in *Jane Eyre* is entirely related to the orchestration of its chronotopes.

Bakhtin goes no further in his identification of the historical influence of chronotopes than the nineteenth century, but he clearly implies that *all* novelistic sub-genres are determined by and can be identified through the particular matrix of chronotopes that frames their narratives. It is not difficult to see the detective novel, the war novel or the campus novel, to take just a few examples, as essentially *chronotopically* constructed. It is perhaps more complex, but no less justified, to conceive of the Modernist novel, which Bakhtin elsewhere approaches – albeit tentatively – in terms of the '*interior infinite*' (RW 44), as a terminal processor of forms of time and as the initiator of a chronotope of its own. It might also be inferred from Bakhtin's analysis that he would have regarded many examples of the *Postmodern* novel as signalling a *reversal* of the gradual emergence of novels of emergence, the ever-increasing ability of literature to 'assimilate real historical time' – as novels defined by an anti-chronotope. In general terms, however, Bakhtin is explicitly clear that chronotopes – and specifically the major chronotopes featured in his discussion – 'lie at the heart of specific varieties of the novel genre' (FTC 252); all sub-genres of the novel are chronotopically defined and can be chronotopically distinguished from one another.

CHRONOTOPE AND HISTORY

Time may be 'the primary category' in the literary chronotope, but this should not lead to the inference that time is somehow *primarily* of interest as it is manifest in and conditions novels. From the outset, as we have seen, Bakhtin frames his analysis as a development of the Kantian proposition that time and space are 'indispensable forms of any cognition, beginning with elementary perceptions and representations' (FTC 85), 'materializing' it and aligning it with his own conception of eventness by insisting that they are also 'forms of the most immediate reality' (FTC 85). In a parallel with the ways in which the concept of heteroglossia facilitates the socialization and historicization of the speech activity of individual subjects (authors, characters and living human beings alike) without generalizing or losing sight of its eventness, the chronotope, too, is conceived as something that is not only – and perhaps not, indeed, primarily – a literary phenomenon. Time may become 'artistically visible' in the literary chronotope, and space responsive to the movements of time and plot, but time and space are the co-ordinates also of *history*. The theory of the chronotope is more than an attempt to concretize literary time; it is an attempt to conceive of history itself in concrete and material terms, but without effacing the value and importance of the particular that such an ostensible generalization might imply.

This is signalled on a number of occasions in the chronotope essay, none perhaps so vivid as Bakhtin's reference to Friedrich Engels' (1820–95) *Dialectics of Nature* (1883) and its declaration that, with the advent of the Renaissance, 'the bounds of the old *orbis terrarum* had been pierced' (Engels 1883; FTC 206). For Engels, a new world was 'discovered', a revolution in consciousness had taken place, which cast every phenomenon – from economic and social relations to literature – in an entirely new light, paving the way for the emergence of the scientific revolution. For Bakhtin, *time itself* had changed; as well as being a part of the frame within which everything else must be understood – the contention from which the chronotope begins – human understanding of time is also subject to cognitive 'framing': time itself was not the same for the ancients as it would be for the bourgeois inhabitants of the eighteenth century or indeed for the inhabitants of the globalized twenty-first century. By the time of Rabelais (and the birth of the modern European novel),

> it was necessary to find a new form of time and a new relationship of time to space […]. A new chronotope was needed that would permit one to link real life (history) to the real earth […] a productive and creative time, a time measured by creativity, by growth and not by destruction.
>
> (FTC 206)

This 'new chronotope', identified by Bakhtin in its *literary* context, is itself a product of the extra-literary environment of the Renaissance and the period immediately thereafter. Just as polyglossia – the birth of a multi-languaged consciousness – altered the nature of language and our understanding of it forever, so too time is 'altered' in the Renaissance to the point where it may be more justified to regard the Renaissance not as a 'period' or a 'cultural revolution', but rather as a *chronotope*. Chronotopes, Bakhtin implies, are such effective ways of analysing the interior of literary texts because those texts emerge from an environment – the sum total of social and ideological forces in play in their time – that is itself profoundly chronotopic. Chronotopes are not therefore only (or even primarily) ways of understanding the literary text; they are also ways of understanding *history*, with history being understood, to return to terms we encountered in Chapter 3, not in a purely abstract (or theoreticist) manner, but in its open, unfinalizable eventness. Only then, and as a consequence of this, do they become fully realized as ways of understanding the literary text *in history*. Chronotopes therefore not only go beyond what Bakhtin dismisses elsewhere as an implicitly superficial 'literary history', they also gesture beyond the traps of determinism and (abstract) generalization into which materialist theories of history are apt to fall (and of which Engels may be identified from Bakhtin's point of view as a significant example).

Just as there are chronotopes of 'the road' or of 'the castle', the temporal coordinates of which determine the nature of a particular literary plot, the sequences of events that are *possible* in that world, the extent of the growth and change undergone by the characters, so too might we imagine, from a historical perspective, that there are chronotopes of the Renaissance, of Victorian Britain, of Colonialism or of late Capitalism. Just as we may identify a 'form of time' in the interior world of the literary text, the condition of possibility for the particular events of that world, so too, after the example of the Renaissance, we might speculate that a certain 'form' or understanding of time is characteristic of historical periods – that is, implicitly, that time (or our understanding of it) is a *variable*. The particular form of time 'operative' in or characteristic of any given period will powerfully condition our understanding of the material objects, events, social relations, etc. pertaining to that period; the condition of possibility for their understanding is not (or should not be) *our own* chronotope, the chronotope of the observer, but the chronotope of the temporal other we contemplate – or, to transpose Bakhtin's model of self-other relations into a temporal key, the architectonically structured relation of one to the other.

If the Renaissance is defined, as suggested above, by the 'invention' of time, by the inauguration of a properly *temporal* consciousness and the initiation of modern openness, the chronotope of Victorian Britain could be seen as the (localized) beginning of the end for 'Renaissance time'. The chronotope of Victorian Britain is defined by a paradoxical temporal overload, a concentration of the scientifically and technologically driven idea of progress to the point where a new, illusory sense of enclosure and 'eternity' once again began to predominate – where a ubiquitous and overdetermined idea of 'progress' had begotten a closed and static world view. The chronotope of Victorian Britain might be said to function as a particular sub-chronotope of the broader chronotope of Colonialism, the realities of Imperial expansion being precisely what is 'cancelled' by the interior time of the sub-chronotope; the spatio-temporal conditioning of the ideology of Colonialism acts as a (chronotopic) frame for the ways in which the spatio-temporal neutralization of the effects of this ideology is accomplished in the 'local' environment. The chronotope of late Capitalism would be defined as a successive stage in this process, in which the tensions between the chronotope of Victorian Britain and the chronotope of Colonialism are universalized, in which stasis passes itself off as movement, in which time itself would appear to have stopped; it is not for nothing that late Capitalism has been described (and not by its detractors) in terms of the 'end of history'.

The literatures of these successive and chronotopically defined periods are therefore *doubly* chronotopic: they are, on one level, an expression of the particular time-space relations that define the environments in which they are produced, and, on another level, they themselves produce their own repertoire of *literary* chronotopes, which express various aspects of the particular 'form of time' that determines the overarching chronotope of their, well, times. Bakhtin once again, as in his earlier discussion of the literary 'utterance' as a specific point in the broad field of dialogized heteroglossia (Chapter 7), implicitly dismantles any hard and fast boundaries that might be imagined to exist between literature and 'life', 'the world' or 'society'; he locates literature, that is, *in history* – but without implying any kind of determinist or reductive relation between them.

CHRONOTOPE AND LANGUAGE

Bakhtin's construction of the theory of the chronotope – whether as a literary or a 'real-world' ideological phenomenon – on the idea of the interrelatedness of space and time as 'forms of the most immediate reality' appears to displace language (discourse) from the central position it had assumed, to such great effect, in the late 1920s and early 1930s. The chronotope, in determining the frame for narrative in terms of its spatial and, more importantly, temporal dimensions, appears to undermine the 'primary' significance of what is said – by narrators and characters alike: it is, at least in the specifically literary context, a sophisticated theory of plot and narrative and thereby relegates the 'stylistics' from which Bakhtin begins in 'Discourse in the Novel' to a position of secondary importance.

In the 'Concluding Remarks' appended to the chronotope essay in 1973 – written some thirty-five years after the original – Bakhtin himself appears troubled by these implications of the chronotope for language and duly seeks to 'correct' them. Referring the reader to Ernst Cassirer's (1874–1934) *The Philosophy of Symbolic Forms*, and particularly his 'analysis of the reflection of time in language' (Cassirer 1965; FTC 251), Bakhtin invites us to draw a parallel between the chronotope's ability to 'materializ[e] time in space' and the fundamentally chronotopic nature of language as a phenomenon in which *time is already and always inscribed*. Just as narratives and genres have been chronotopically 'formed and developed over the course of many centuries', so too 'any and every literary image is chronotopic':

> Language, as a treasure-house of images, is fundamentally chronotopic. The internal form of the word – the mediating sign through which primary spatial meanings are transferred to temporal relationships (in the broadest sense) – is also chronotopic.
>
> (FTC 252)

Language, like any other aspect of literary form/content or of social life, cannot have been immune from the chronotopic determinations that are, in a sense, the story of its evolution (we might be forgiven for imagining a 'chronotope of polyglossia', for example).

Language is as fundamentally chronotopic as literary genre, Bakhtin argues, because it is possible also to 'see' time in language; more than that, it is impossible to conceive of what Bakhtin has earlier called 'living language' without a sensitivity to its chronotopicity, at the macro- and microcosmic levels.

The practical, 'literary' basis for this parallel can be found in Bakhtin's remarks on Goethe's ability to 'see' the past of the town of Einbeck (BSHR 32) and Honoré de Balzac's (1799–1850) ability 'to "see" time in space' (FTC 247). In what is, incidentally, a suggestive parallel with Freud's analogy between memory and the evolution of the city of Rome (Freud 2004; 'nothing is lost', as Freud says), Goethe is not interested in the 'ghosts' of the past, the 'inanimate, if picturesque ruin that has no essential connection with the living present surrounding it and has no influence on it', but rather the '*essential* and *living* vestige of the past in the present' (BSHR 32). Similarly, Balzac's status as 'great realist' depends for Bakhtin on such characteristics as his ability to depict houses 'as materialized history', to depict 'streets, cities, rural landscapes at the level where they are being worked on by time and history' (FTC 247). Language, Bakhtin now argues, is essentially the same: in every moment of its use, we are able to 'see' the historical processes that have acted upon it over centuries; the more complex the literary image, the more 'visible' the historical processes inscribed in it will become.

The proposition that language itself is 'fundamentally chronotopic' invokes two important aspects of Bakhtin's thought that are absent from the chronotope essay at the level of explicit discussion: the first is his core theorization of the embodied subject in the eventness of his or her being, acting and speaking from his or her own unique and non-reiterable location (and moment) in being; the second is the necessary supplementation of that core idea by the mature theory of language as a social, heteroglot phenomenon we saw in the previous chapter. In relation to the first, the chronotope is a way of reiterating that the individual can only ever occupy *this* space and *this* time and therefore underlines the unique, non-reiterable quality of his or her utterance. In relation to the second, the chronotope provides a frame for understanding the discursive nature of the class, social grouping, generation, etc. from which and in dialogue with which the individual utterance is made and forms its stylistic and semantic profile. This relationship might now be understood in precisely the same way as Bakhtin has described (literary) chronotopes as 'mutually inclusive', 'co-exist[ent]' and 'interwoven'; they 'replace or oppose one another, contradict one another or find themselves in ever more complex interrelationships' (FTC 252). Bakhtin's theory of discourse is, in essence, restated in terms of the chronotope:

> The general characteristic of [...] interactions [among and within chronotopes] is that they are *dialogical* (in the broadest sense of the word).
>
> (FTC 252)

We may view this as convincing evidence of the unity of Bakhtin's thought as a whole, or as a belated attempt to efface the contradictions between two incommensurable points of view. In the latter case, the problem is that Bakhtin, having dispensed with theories of the 'image' in his earlier work, now reinstates the image as necessary for the reconciliation of the chronotope with language; or, in other words, he assumes – or insists – that 'seeing' time in language is essentially no different from 'seeing' time in space. In both cases, however, whether we prefer to read Bakhtin's reconciliation of the chronotope with language as evidence of unity or of contradiction, the value and utility of the chronotope as an analytical category is not diminished.

SUMMARY

On one level, the chronotope is a way of describing and categorizing the different forms of space-time relations that are manifest in literary texts and that, for Bakhtin, determine the genre to which a work belongs. At different points in the historical development of literature, different and distinct 'forms of time' have predominated, from the 'adventure-time' of the Greek novel to the 'real historical time' of modern, realist literature; it is the ability in fact to assimilate real historical time that determines the power and pre-eminence of the realist novel. Plot, character development, and even language itself are profoundly chronotopic; the particular chronotope of a novel determines its limits and possibilities in relation to the representation of events, concepts and ideology. The *Bildungsroman* is the most straightforward example of generic definition in chronotopic terms, but Bakhtin emphasizes the simultaneous presence and interaction of a range of chronotopes in a single work, from the chronotope of the idyll to the chronotope of the road. On another level, the chronotope functions as a way of conceiving of the narrative(s) of history beyond – but not separate from – the literary text and the history of literature. It is therefore a restatement of the core Bakhtinian proposition of the inseparability of literature from its social and ideological environment, which, like the concept of heteroglossia, guarantees at the same time that one cannot somehow be reduced to the other. It is also cognate with the key idea of unfinalizability, which, once again in a parallel with heteroglossia, is transposed through the chronotope from the level of the particular to the level of the generalized or even 'universal' – without becoming abstracted and losing the force of its eventness in the process.

NOTE

1 The published English translation prefers 'evolution' to 'becoming'.

9

CARNIVAL

The idea of *carnival* and the related *carnivalization* emerge from Bakhtin's reading of the popular folk culture of the Middle Ages and its transmission in the Renaissance, the subject of his book *Rabelais and His World* (largely written in the late 1930s and 1940s, published in Russian in 1965, and published in English translation in 1968). In one important sense, carnival is deeply reflective of Bakhtin's thought as a whole, developing the key ideas of embodiment and unfinalizability to an almost poetic extreme (for which Bakhtin has often been criticized). The Rabelais book is therefore most obviously related to the essay on the chronotope, elaborating on its emphasis of *becoming*, the insistence that nothing is more significant than the resistance to closure, the unfinalizability of the human subject, the question and process of '*how a person becomes other*' (FTC 115). It might even be argued that, where the chronotope essay has focused on *time* as the 'primary category' (FTC 85), the Rabelais book revisits the same set of problems by now prioritizing 'the material bodily principle' (RW 19), pursuing all the implications of embodied, participative life as a basis for an explicitly 'materialistic concept of being' (RW 52). Time is not absent from carnival – otherwise it could not produce the development, the becoming that is required for renewal and rebirth (unfinalizability) – but in carnival as an actualized 'ritual spectacle', it is suspended; it cedes its primary role to the bodily inhabitation of carnival space, a theme to which we will return later in this chapter.

On a different level, however, carnival shares another characteristic with the chronotope, one that guarantees it a somewhat curious status in Bakhtin's thought. While undoubtedly a significant Bakhtinian concept – perhaps even the most recognizable and influential of them all – carnival, like the chronotope, emerges *after* the linguistic turn that drives a fundamental shift in Bakhtin's thought in the late 1920s; and, like the chronotope, carnival does not derive from or depend upon a theory of language. In both carnival and the chronotope, albeit in differing degrees, the figure of Rabelais embodies and exemplifies a qualitative shift in European literature in terms of the 'fullness' of the spatio-temporal *image* of both character and history (character-in-history) it is equipped to represent. In Bakhtin's theory of the chronotope, however, language, as we have seen, is ultimately re-inscribed into his conceptual system; in the theory of carnival, this is at the very least arguable, and language appears to remain secondary to 'the material bodily principle' and to *laughter*, which emerges as a unique form of mediation between the body (material being) and the mind (verbal embodiment).

Carnival, like the chronotope, might ultimately be seen as a transposition of Bakhtin's core programme, a variation on a theme; it might equally be viewed as standing apart from Bakhtin's work as a whole. Notwithstanding its potential relations with the remainder of Bakhtin's work, carnival is the most self-sufficient or 'portable' of Bakhtin's concepts, capable of standing (or falling) in isolation, perhaps because it is also the most thoroughly *topical* or even *occasional* of all his ideas. Carnival belongs to and is determined by the time and circumstances in which it was elaborated to a greater extent than anything else Bakhtin produced.

This chapter will deal briefly with the immediate context in which carnival emerged in the course of outlining its basic coordinates, before examining how carnival becomes carnivalization, the principle of laughter that lies at its heart, and the dominant mode of a 'carnivalized' literature, namely grotesque realism; it will conclude by returning to the context outlined above in order to consider in greater detail the significance of the body in carnival.

THE CONTEXT(S) OF CARNIVAL

The term 'carnival' initially refers to the actual practice of 'ritual spectacle' in which the people of the Middle Ages actively participated (as opposed to one in which they were purely spectators), and which, Bakhtin tells us, occupied as much as three months of the year in certain medieval European cities (RW 13). These carnival festivals were 'non-official, extra-ecclesiastical and extra-political [...] a second world and a second life outside officialdom' (RW 6); their purpose was to oppose official truth, 'a truth already established, the predominant truth that was put forward as eternal and undisputable' (RW 9). In carnival, 'real' life was suspended or turned upside-down; carnival was a 'second life' of the people, 'organized on the basis of laughter', and dedicated to 'the world's renewal and revival' (RW 8, 7).

The practice of carnival gradually diminished during the Renaissance, became increasingly licensed by state authorities, and, eventually, in the seventeenth and eighteenth centuries was 'transformed into a mere holiday mood' (RW 33). The 'spirit' of carnival, however, was not lost in the process; it is, Bakhtin insists, 'indestructible' (RW 33). Instead, it increasingly found expression in literature. Literature, and around it entire cultures, was in other words *carnivalized*; the carnival spirit, over centuries, broke out from the market square, where it was increasingly denied expression. The carnival of the Middle Ages not only lived on in European literature from the Renaissance to the twentieth century, it became a significant – but barely noticed – agent of change and re-animation of literature and literary genres (Bakhtin is even willing to build a version of European literary history around the carnival principle). The fulcrum of this alternative literary history is Bakhtin's analysis of Rabelais, who represents the key idea that the Renaissance was not a clean break with the medieval past, but rather a 'crossroads' at which 'the [earlier] folk culture of humour' meets and conditions aspects of the subsequent 'bourgeois conception of the completed atomized being' (RW 24). Carnival and carnivalization are driven by the central conviction that the culture of the Middle Ages – 'folk', collective and ambivalent – has been surreptitiously transmitted (through literature) to the culture of Modernity – which Bakhtin identifies as (predominantly) 'official', individualistic and rational.

This reference to a 'rational', 'official culture' invites immediate reflection on the topicality of carnival, to which we have referred above. The years in which carnival consistently occupied Bakhtin, from the late 1930s until 1950 (leaving aside a brief spell later on), span the grotesque peak of Stalin's repression in 1937, the cataclysmic period of the Second World War, and the obscure and gloomily repressive postwar years of late Stalinism. The loss of hundreds of thousands of lives during 'peacetime' before and after the War was punctuated only by the War's acceleration of the deaths, now 'legal', into the tens of millions. Bakhtin, throughout this period, lived a peripatetic existence between Moscow and various provincial towns, preoccupied with the day-to-day imperatives of his own livelihood, including, before and after the War, attempts to obtain higher degrees on the basis of what would later become *Rabelais and His World*. Certain aspects of the book – and perhaps its overall thesis – must therefore be read in the context of this period.

It is difficult, for example, not to see the official culture of Stalinism, with its choreographed displays of ideological adherence in various forms of official 'spectacle', as the immediate context for such generalizations, ostensibly referring to the seventeenth and eighteenth centuries, as 'the state encroached upon festive life and turned it into a parade' (RW 33), or, ostensibly in relation to the Middle Ages, as

the official feast looked back at the past and used the past to consecrate the present [...] it asserted all that was stable, unchanging, perennial: the existing hierarchy, the existing religious, political and moral values. It was the triumph of a truth already established [...].

(RW 9)

Bakhtin's reference to carnival's distinction from 'political *cult* forms and ceremonials' (RW 5, my emphasis) explicitly characterizes carnival in opposition to the cult of Stalin's personality that had been the central purpose of the 'official ceremonial' of the time, but which had been exposed and (partially) rejected following Stalin's death in 1953. By the time of the book's publication in 1965, the Soviet reader could be in no doubt as to the object of such a remark.

SOCIALIST REALISM

State control of Soviet cultural life under Stalin took the form not simply of control over publishing, broadcasting, education, and literature and the arts through a combination of direct state-controlled administration and primary censorship, but also of the promulgation of official state doctrines in literature and the arts, and in many branches of both Science and the Humanities. The doctrine of *Socialist Realism* was adopted as official state policy for literature and the arts in 1934, requiring writers and artists to depict not only 'reality', but also 'a historically concrete representation of reality in its revolutionary development'. Partly because of its own instability and incoherence – the concept of realism having generated sufficient contradictions, even without the admixture of the 'historically concrete' and 'revolutionary development' – and partly because it became a convenient device through which the state could direct literature and the arts in line with the political imperative of the day, Socialist Realism produced a largely static and, indeed, finalized art. Its one-dimensional images of optimistic progress towards a 'bright future' in fact contrasted with the closed, repressive, authoritarian realities of Soviet life and culture. The literary, critical, cultural and social environment of the 1930s and late 1940s contrasts vividly with the open, evolving culture of growth and fertility Bakhtin attributes to Rabelais and 'his world'.

It is equally difficult not to interpret Bakhtin's concept of *grotesque realism*, which we will later deal with at greater length, as a deliberate counter to the 'official' artistic doctrine of Stalin's Soviet Union, so-called 'socialist realism', with its one-dimensional images of 'Soviet man' as, precisely, 'determined, predetermined, bygone and finished, that is, essentially not living' (TPA 9) – *finalized*. When Bakhtin writes of the carnival principle as 'indestructible', of the redemptive power of 'folk laughter', of the 'fearlessness' of folk culture in the face of the terror of the world (RW 39), of the collective 'ancestral body of the people' (RW 29), it is difficult not to hear a prayer that the collective body – the people – will survive its threatened annihilation. As Bakhtin explicitly acknowledges,

Rabelais and His World, in its determination to oppose 'the triumph of a truth already established', is suffused with a *utopianism* that, while certainly present in the remainder of his work, never quite becomes as dominant, in tone or in conceptual content. The pronounced and explicit utopian dimension of carnival derives from the Soviet – and Bakhtin's own – experience of Stalinism.

CARNIVAL, CARNIVALIZATION AND LAUGHTER

Carnival as 'ritual spectacle' in the Middle Ages was above all 'non-official', a licensed time out of life, a 'temporary liberation from the prevailing truth and the established order' (RW 10). During carnival, 'all hierarchical rank, privileges, norms and prohibitions' were suspended (RW 10); life was lived 'inside out', a fact symbolized by the prominent role of comic crownings and uncrownings (the carnival king/fool). The function of carnival was (for a time, at least):

> [to oppose] all that was ready-made and completed, [...] to liberate from the prevailing point of view of the world, from conventions and established truths, from clichés, from all that is humdrum and universally accepted.
>
> (RW 11, 34)

The resonances with the concept of unfinalizability and, related to it, the central idea of the 'eventness' of meaning, its live creation in the process of dialogic interaction, are explicitly clear. Official (monologic) culture maintains the 'pretense' that truth and knowledge are 'stable, unchanging, perennial [...] eternal and undisputable' (RW 9); carnival 'liberates' not by somehow overturning the official culture or the (political) authority on which it rests, but rather by maintaining – actualizing, embodying – the principle that *nothing* is 'stable, unchanging, perennial [...] eternal and undisputable', that nothing is finalized, that everything is in a constant state of change: 'nothing conclusive has yet taken place in the world [...] the world is open and free, everything is still in the future and will always be in the future' (PDP 166), as Bakhtin has expressed it in his book on Dostoevsky. For as long as carnival (or the 'carnival spirit') exists outside of and in opposition to official culture and political authority, it will remind authority that it is not eternal or immune to change – that other forces exist outside and independent of it and that it, too, must pass. This is why criticism of carnival for its lack of political agency, its provision of a temporary release that ultimately *entrenches* what it opposes, is wide of the mark. This type of criticism parallels (and perhaps derives from) Herbert Marcuse's (1898–1979) criticism that the apparently radical work of art, by its very existence, in the end legitimizes rather than undermines the political and economic structures of the environment in which it is produced (Marcuse 1968). Carnival existed not as a form of agency, but as a reminder that agency was possible.

As carnival gradually became licensed, incorporated into the 'official' calendar, it was, as Bakhtin admits, increasingly 'transformed into a mere holiday mood [...] into a parade' (RW 33). The consequences and significance of this loss of force are anticipated, however, in Bakhtin's insistence from the outset that carnival, even in its originary form as an actualized ritual spectacle, 'belongs to the borderline between art and life'. It is a 'real-life' phenomenon, but one that is 'shaped according to a certain pattern', which, like the ritual of the church, anticipates its own later transformation into the forms of art (RW 7). When carnival ceases to be carnival on the public square, it renews itself by finding a vehicle in various literary forms – transforming and renewing those forms in the process. The carnival spirit, which is indestructible, finds in the period of the Renaissance new means of survival and is 'transmitted as a now purely literary tradition' (RW 34).

The form Bakhtin first identifies as receptive to or determined by the carnival spirit (just as it was in relation to polyglossia, heteroglossia and the novel) is *parody*, the closest formal equivalent to the 'comic crownings and uncrownings' of the actual carnival. Carnivalistic parody is nonetheless

> far distant from the negative and formal parody of modern times. Folk humour denies, but it revives and renews at the same time. Bare negation is completely alien to folk culture.
>
> (RW 11)

Festival or carnival laughter is *ambivalent*, 'it is also directed at those who laugh' (RW 12). The 'folk', in rejecting the finalized, 'triumphant' truth of official culture, do not pretend to a finalized, indisputable truth of their own; it might therefore be said, but for the essentially non-verbal nature of this ambivalent carnival laughter, that it, too, is *double-voiced* – that carnival laughter is dialogic.

Similarly, satire may be a carrier for the carnival spirit, as long as the satirist does not indulge in a one-dimensionally *negative* laughter which 'places him above the object of his mockery' (RW 12). Carnival, we recall, is something that must be *participated* in, rather than spectated upon ('it has no footlights' (RW 7), as Bakhtin expresses it in a suggestive rejection of a certain type of theatre). Literary forms of whichever kind are potentially receptive to the ambivalent influence of the carnival spirit and carnival laughter; but their *form* – their surface, compositional form – as we have seen in relation to Dostoevsky (Chapter 6) and to the novel generally (Chapter 7), is not the decisive factor. At the level of deep, architectonic form, which is determined by the relations between the consciousnesses that intersect in the literary work, one parody or satire may be profoundly carnivalistic (or dialogic), while others are just as profoundly monologic – constructed on the basis of 'bare negation'.

Satire and parody, the key means by which literature is carnivalized, are also, of course, the leading examples of the 'parodic-travestying literature' we dealt with in Chapter 6, which exposes monologic discourse as 'one-sided, bounded, incapable of exhausting its object' (PND 55), and which can proliferate only 'under the condition of thoroughgoing polyglossia' (PND 61). Parody, in particular, driven by the global force of polyglossia, helped 'liberate [...] the object from the power of language [...]; free [...] consciousness from the power of the direct word' (PND 60); yet it does so, quite specifically, by introducing 'the permanent corrective of laughter' (PND 55). Laughter, in other words, in parallel with the inter-animation of languages initiated by polyglossia, is a key factor also in the organization of the *representation of language*. Laughter is another name for the conditions of possibility of double-voiced discourse. The denial of laughter is equivalent to the (illusory) denial of the double-voiced nature of discourse.

In literature, therefore, laughter does not equate with the comic, but is identified wherever the one-sided seriousness of any discourse is exposed to the light of another, questioning consciousness;

through literary laughter, outsideness is brought inside; it becomes immanent in the text itself. In 'Forms of Time and of the Chronotope in the Novel', for example, the 'autobiographical expression of a singular self-consciousness' of the earliest memoir literature gives way to a 'satirico-ironic or humorous representation of oneself and one's life in satires and diatribes' (FTC 143, 293); or the figures of the clown, the rogue and the fool – quintessential carnival figures – are present in literature not simply to entertain, but to facilitate the introduction into literature of the 'prosaic metaphor', which for Bakhtin covers all forms of 'parody', 'joke', 'humour', 'irony', 'grotesque' and 'whimsy' (FTC 166). The prosaic metaphor, although it is not the explicit *linguistic* focus in the Rabelais book, is essentially discourse structured by laughter – double-voiced discourse by any other name. The (surface) 'formal' dimension is once again not of primary significance. When Bakhtin turns to Rabelais in search of a 'crossroads' exemplar of how literary form(s) are both receptive to and transformed and renewed by the 'ambivalent' essence of carnival, he relies not on isolated 'formal' descriptions such as parody – or even novel – but on a particular mode of representation or aesthetic principle that covers them all, which derives from the folk-carnival culture of the Middle Ages and which largely determines the 'non-official' course of European literary history – *grotesque realism*.

GROTESQUE REALISM

Grotesque realism is, essentially, the dominant manifestation of the carnival spirit in literature and culture after the demise of carnival as a maximally free ritual spectacle. Rabelais, for Bakhtin, is the writer who establishes grotesque realism as a live force in the development of European literature, its 'purest and most consistent representative' (RW 30). Consistent with carnival's 'decrownings', its celebration of life lived upside down or inside out:

> The essential principle of grotesque realism is degradation, that is, the lowering of all that is high, spiritual, ideal, abstract; it is a transfer to the material level, to the sphere of earth and body in their indissoluble unity.
>
> (RW 18–9)

To degrade in carnival is not, however, an entirely negative act; it is the necessary precondition for rebirth and renewal. Death and decay relate to birth and growth precisely in terms of 'indissoluble unity', for one is inseparably present in the other:

> Degradation digs a bodily grave for a new birth; it has not only a destructive, negative aspect, but also a regenerating one. To degrade an object does not imply merely hurling it into the void of non-existence, into absolute destruction, but to hurl it down to the reproductive lower stratum, the zone in which conception and a new birth take place. Grotesque realism knows no other level; it is the fruitful earth and womb. It is always conceiving.
>
> (RW 21)

Bakhtin's first example of the carnival grotesque image in literature after Rabelais is the paired image of Sancho Panza and Don Quixote. Sancho's

> potbelly, appetite, his abundant defecation, are on the absolute lower level of grotesque realism of the gay bodily grave (belly, bowels, earth) which has been dug for Don Quixote's abstract and deadened idealism.
>
> (RW 22)

Yet, this is already in itself a relatively 'degraded' carnival grotesque image. For a pure expression of the carnival grotesque, this time long before Rabelais, Bakhtin reaches back to the fourth-century-B.C. terracotta figurines discovered at Kerch on the Crimean Peninsula depicting 'senile pregnant hags', who are, moreover, 'laughing' (RW 25):

> They combine a senile, decaying and deformed body with the body of new life, conceived but as yet unformed. Life is shown here as an ambivalent, internally contradictory process. There is nothing complete; this is unfinalizability in its purest form.
>
> (RW 25–6)

The Kerch figurines, Sancho Panza and Don Quixote, and Gargantua and Pantagruel, are parodic, but not in the narrow sense: all facilitate the representation of

> a phenomenon in a state of transformation, an as yet unfinalized meta-
> morphosis, in the stages of its death and birth, growth and becoming.
>
> (RW 24)

Rabelais (a 'crossroads' figure) guarantees that such representations
will not only survive the Renaissance, but that, after him,

> the entire field of realistic literature [...] is strewn with the fragments of
> grotesque realism, which at times are not mere remnants of the past, but
> manifest a renewed vitality.
>
> (RW 24)

Modern European literature, at times surreptitiously, at others
more explicitly, has been thoroughly carnivalized under the enduring
influence of grotesque realism.

The clue to the terminal point in this process, as well as to the
ways in which it relates to Bakhtin's earlier work, is his insistence
that 'the grotesque image never had [...] a canon. It is non-canonical'
(RW 30); in pursuit of 'the inner movement of being itself [...] the
eternal incompleteness of being' (RW 32), it works to break down
the 'boundaries' between the phenomena it encounters, including
form. As well as evoking Bakhtin's celebrated claim that 'the cultural domain has no inner territory: it is entirely located on
boundaries, and boundaries intersect its every element [...]'
(PCMF 274), this also gestures towards the literary form that will
dominate and eventually 'complete' this process, the ultimate non-
canonical, boundary-effacing phenomenon of European literature
since Rabelais – the novel. Bakhtin opens the essay 'Epic and
Novel' with the claim that 'the novel is the only genre still in a
state of becoming, still unfinished [...] younger than writing and
the book' (EN 3), it does not possess 'defined generic contours' (EN
4) and is therefore uniquely able to disrupt and absorb into itself
through parody and stylization all other genres, which entered the
modern era as forms that have been already fixed (EN 4). It is
opposed to the 'epic', an 'absolutely finished and completed generic
form', defined chronotopically in terms of an 'absolute past', which
'lacks any relativity' (EN 15); its separation from subsequent times
is a 'boundary [...] immanent in the form of the epic itself' (EN
16). In other words, the novel is receptive to and a carrier for the

carnival grotesque – which might be said to be 'immanent' in the form of the novel itself – while the epic (and perhaps all non-novelistic literary forms) is a genre of the finalization and the sanctity of all boundaries, which abhors transgression, ambivalence, free and familiar contact, and becoming. Like the official festival, epic 'use[s] the past to consecrate the present' (RW 9); it is 'immanently' resistant to the carnival grotesque.

Bakhtin has closed 'Discourse in the Novel' not with the opposition novel-epic, but rather with a discussion of 'two stylistic lines' in the development of the novel itself. That distinction is driven by the terms that drive 'Discourse in the Novel' as a whole and which we have earlier identified as being absent from *Rabelais and His World*, namely the social stratification of language and dialogized heteroglossia. Yet, in a parallel that suggests that carnival is a consistent and integral element of Bakhtin's thought, as opposed to a creative digression, his discussion of the stylistic bifurcation in the history of the novel could without much alteration be replayed in terms of receptivity to the carnival spirit and grotesque realism. The novel – or rather 'novelness' – is carnivalesque; the modern novel is the final endpoint of the history of European literature retold as a history of grotesque realism.

THE BODY IN CARNIVAL

If Bakhtin's carnival restaging of the story of how Western culture since the Renaissance has descended into abstract reified monologism, and of how the novel is the agent and manifestation of resistance to this process, can largely function *without* language, we have already glimpsed what will 'replace' language in this account. Where earlier his ideas on the eventness of being and the architectonics of self-other relations have collided with a theory of language (discourse) to produce what might rather awkwardly be termed a theory of 'embodiment in language', in *Rabelais and His World* embodiment cedes its literal status to something altogether more figurative. Bakhtin here offers a theory not of embodiment as it has appeared in his thought to date, but of the carnival body – which is essentially a symbolic body.

The body is essential both for carnival itself (as ritual spectacle of the Middle Ages) and for the carnival symbolic, the images that migrate to later culture and literature. Carnival, as we have seen, involved bodily participation, 'a special form of free and familiar contact' between people 'who were usually divided by barriers of caste, property, profession, and age'; carnival was above all 'experienced' (RW 10). In carnival, the individual participates with his or her body in something that is founded on the principle of that body's subsumption into something larger than itself, the 'collective ancestral body' of the people (RW 19). In Rabelais, in direct reflection of this, 'the material bodily principle, that is, images of the human body with its food, defecation, and sexual life, plays a predominant role'; this 'material bodily principle' is the 'heritage [...] of the culture of folk humour' (RW 18). In Rabelais, however, who is the key point of mediation between the culture of folk humour and a portable carnival symbolic, 'images of the body are offered [...] in an extremely exaggerated form' (RW 18); in grotesque realism in general, the body in question is not merely 'the body and its physiology in the modern sense', the 'individualized' body of a 'biological individual' with a 'bourgeois ego', but the body of

the people, a people who are continually growing and renewed. This is why all that is bodily becomes grandiose, exaggerated, immeasurable. This exaggeration has a positive, assertive character. The leading themes of these images of bodily life are fertility, growth, and a brimming-over abundance. Manifestations of this life refer not to the isolated biological individual, not to the private, egotistic 'economic man', but to the collective ancestral body.

(RW 19)

Exaggeration and overemphasis are indices of *value*; the greater the scale of the body's ingestion and copulation, the greater its value. Just as time is the primary measure of scale in the chronotope, so corporeal size and physical vitality are the primary indicators of value in the carnival symbolic.

The body in the carnival symbolic does not in fact coincide with the body as any kind of totality, but is concentrated, as we have begun to see, in what Bakhtin terms 'the lower bodily stratum' – the belly, bowels and reproductive organs. This is, at the most literal level, because it is in the lower bodily stratum that renewal and rebirth actually take place; but it is also because these organs, like the nose and the mouth, in development of the above point about the grotesque predilection for the transgression and effacement of all boundaries, emphasize that

> the grotesque body is not separated from the rest of the world; it is not closed, it is unfinalized, unfinished, it outgrows itself, transgresses its own limits. Those parts of the body that are open to the outside world are accentuated, the parts through which the world enters the body or emerges from it [...] The body discloses its essence as a principle of growth which exceeds its own limits only in such acts as copulation, pregnancy, child-birth, the throes of death, eating, drinking, or defecation. [...] The unfinished and open body (dying, giving birth, and being born) is not separated from the world by clearly defined boundaries; it is blended with the world [...] The body represents and embodies the material bodily world as the absolute lower stratum.
>
> (RW 26-7)

This explains the gulf between modern 'vulgarity' and the ambivalent, perhaps even double-voiced, nature of swearing and abuse in folk humour: where 'modern indecent abuse and cursing' – much like 'the negative and formal parody of modern times' – 'have retained dead and purely negative remnants of the grotesque concept of the body', carnival abuse not only sends its object 'down to the absolute lower bodily stratum, to the zone of the genital organs, the bodily grave', it does so in order then to regenerate and renew it (RW 28). In the modern 'private sphere of isolated individuals', the lower bodily stratum has preserved 'the element of negation, while losing almost entirely [its] positive regenerating force' (RW 23).

The 'positive regenerating force' of the lower bodily stratum, while it is a component of the carnival symbolic in general terms, is also a site of direct signification; here, laughter (actual, bodily laughter) distinguishes itself from speech. The body in carnival does not spend too much time speaking, and the function of the mouth in the carnival symbolic is associated more with eating and swearing than with speech; but laughter, as an embodied physiological act, facilitates a signification in and of the body. Laughter for Bakhtin may be omnipresent in medieval folk culture in general, but it is explicitly, physiologically present in carnival. Laughter is explicitly identified with the 'material-bodily origin' (RW 80); like spitting, swearing, eating and drinking, farting, and defecating, laughter is an explicitly *expressive* bodily function, performed by the body in carnival in embodiment of the rejection of authority, as well as in celebration of the body's openness and potential for growth. The expressive nature of carnival laughter, in its literal and performed sense, can be approached by recalling Voloshinov's core conceptualization of the sign. The verbal sign, in particular, is distinct from other signs because it exists precisely in order to signify (MPL 14); other *visual* signs (for example, the hammer and sickle, bread and wine) refer in the first instance to material objects, which already exist and perform other non-signifying functions, and are 'transformed into' or reused as signs (MPL 9). Eating and drinking, although they undoubtedly signify in Rabelais, remain more closely associated with their 'primary' physiological function of sustaining life than, for example, spitting, whose physiological function is almost entirely utilized for the purpose of signification. Swearing is much closer to the verbal sign proper, although with a strong emphasis on basic physiological function (in its performance and in its content). Laughter emerges in this analysis as an almost perfect combination of the bodily and the signifying: it is the embodiment and at the same time the expression of the 'material-bodily origin', emphasizing its resilience, its life force and its capacity for survival and regeneration – its *fearlessness* (RW 39). It is therefore the perfect expression of embodiment in the Bakhtinian sense, and, in its opposition to 'all that is finished and polished' (RW 3), it reaffirms the similarly axiomatic point that unfinalizability is in no sense contrary to embodiment.

SUMMARY

Derived from the ritual spectacle of the Middle Ages, *carnival* is Bakhtin's distillation of the spirit of the 'non-official', 'second life of the people' in its opposition to any conception of truth as eternal and indisputable. Carnival is a symbolic shorthand for openness, growth and potential in opposition to closure and reification, to all that is 'ready-made and completed', and is hence closely related to the concept of *unfinalizability*. In post-Renaissance European culture, the carnival spirit survives in literature, which is *carnivalized* in the process. Bakhtin's key exemplar of the moment of transmission is Rabelais, particularly his *Gargantua and Pantagruel*. The key mode of a carnivalized literature is *grotesque realism*, which seeks to incorporate and reconceive the parodic-travestying forms that have been so central to both *dialogized heteroglossia* and the *chronotope*; the images of grotesque realism combine degradation and renewal, death and rebirth – an affirmative negation. Carnival is related to the remainder of Bakhtin's work in ways that reflect this core ambivalence: on one hand, it represents a departure, displacing language from the central position it has occupied since the late 1920s in favour of a more pronounced focus on laughter and the materiality of the body (*embodiment*, now without language); on the other hand, it is a reinscription of double-voicedness and the dialogic, which recasts the unique properties of the novel and novelness in the specific terms of the carnivalesque and grotesque realism.

10

GENRE

Genre is at once the most elusive concept in Bakhtin and one of the most productive, drawing together as it does – albeit sometimes into relations of conflict – aspects of all of his key ideas. This combination of elusiveness and productivity results primarily from the sense in which genre is in Bakhtin's hands both a definitively literary category and at the same time expressive of the seamless unity of the literary and non-literary he has pursued throughout his work. Another difficulty lies in the fact that at different points in time Bakhtin (and Medvedev) offer no less than five different, but related, theories of genre, from Medvedev's initial theorization in the 1920s, through theories that are related to the categories of the novel, chronotope and carnival we have already discussed, to the 'conclusive' theory of genre Bakhtin builds around the idea of *speech genres* in the 1950s. This chapter will outline (and in some cases revisit) each of these five theories of genre in turn, beginning with Medvedev and digressing to assess the sense in which the very idea of genre appears at certain points to be in danger of collapsing under the weight of the theoretical work it is required to do. It will conclude by examining the implications of speech genres for the idea of 'literature' itself.

CONDITIONS OF PERFORMANCE
AND PERCEPTION

The theory of genre proposed in Medvedev's *The Formal Method in Literary Scholarship: A Critical Introduction to Sociological Poetics* is intended as a corrective, once again, to the approach to genre of the Russian Formalists, which is airily (and unfairly) dismissed as being 'mechanically assembled from devices' (FM 129). Medvedev insists instead that the genre of a given literary work is determined by two factors, which are so closely related as to be virtually inseparable: first, every literary work is orientated towards a reader and towards 'definite conditions of performance and perception' (FM 131); second, 'the work is oriented in life from within, so to speak, by its thematic content' (FM 131). Medvedev's description of 'conditions of performance and perception' may already seem very familiar:

> The work enters real space and time, it is loud or silent, it is associated with the church or with the stage, or with the music-hall; it may be part of a festival or simply a part of leisure. The work presupposes a particular audience of listeners or readers, a particular means for their reaction, a particular kind of interrelation between the audience and the author. [...] the work enters into life and comes into contact with various aspects of its surrounding reality in the process of its actual realization as something performed, heard, read at a particular time, in a particular place, and in particular circumstances. [...] All variations of the dramatic, lyric and epic genres are determined by this unmediated orientation of discourse as a fact or, more precisely, as something which is historically accomplished in the context of its surrounding reality.
>
> (FM 131)

The work is therefore like the utterance: its meaning cannot in any way be divorced from the location and moment in which it is produced or from the listener/audience to which it is addressed.

Theme, on the other hand, relates to everything evoked in the work itself, its range of human and inanimate objects, as well as to the ideas expressed in it (its 'themes' in the narrow or conventional sense) and the events it represents; but, just as the utterance acquires its full meaning only as the utterance of an embodied subject in the particular, once-occurrent event of its enunciation, so too the theme of the work cannot be said to 'mean' anything in isolation from the actual conditions of its performance and perception:

> The theme of the work is the theme of the whole utterance as a specifically defined socio-historical act. It follows, therefore, that theme is just as inseparable from the entire situation of the utterance as it is from its linguistic elements. [...] The thematic unity of the work and its actual place in life grow together organically in the unity of genre. [...] Genre is the organic unity of theme and of what lies beyond it.
>
> (FM 132–3)

Different genres – and indeed different art forms – have different ways of finalizing the materials from which they are made, which are as much determined by their actual place in the world as by the formal means at their disposal – in fact, more so.

Medvedev would appear in this to anticipate the idea later proposed by the Canadian critic Northrop Frye (1912–91), who distinguishes genres in terms of the 'radical of presentation' that originally brought them into being: epic, for example, is defined in terms of its having been sung or chanted to a *present* audience (Frye 1957: 246). The difference is that Frye is interested in an archetypal base for genre, according to which genres themselves become the primary factor in determining genre – later 'epics' conform to (in greater degree) or diverge from (in lesser degree) a foundational template, the form of which has been established in its 'originary' moment (albeit a moment that must always be imagined or surmised), the canonic example of which is Homer's *Iliad* (760–710 B.C.). For Medvedev (and Bakhtin and Voloshinov), the immediate 'conditions of performance and perception' are not only paramount, they are also implicitly *knowable*. Generic conventions and 'expectations' do indeed become *part* of these conditions as time progresses, but they cannot predominate over the immediate architectonics of the event of a particular work. The work remains an utterance: our perspective on its (generic) relations to other utterances (works) must begin with its *own* conditions of performance and perception.

Medvedev's theory is closely related to many aspects of Bakhtin's thought as a whole. It parallels the core definition of the dialogic we encountered in Chapter 6, the sense in which the word is 'formed' in a dual process of encountering, first, its *object* and, second, an anticipated *response* (which map neatly onto 'theme' and 'conditions of performance and perception'). It also provides a practical model for some of the ideas we examined in Chapter 5 in relation to Voloshinov's insistence on the definitively social dimension of discourse: the work conceived of as a 'whole utterance as speech performance' (FM 132) invites the conclusion that genre, too, is profoundly conditioned by 'social evaluation' – it is, in the 'organic unity' of theme and conditions of performance and perception, a profoundly socio-historical phenomenon. It conforms in large measure to the demands of a dialogical approach and, like Voloshinov's theory of the utterance, conceives of literature in close relation to the world of discourse beyond the specifically literary.

THE NOVEL (AGAIN)

The problem with Medvedev's theory of genre, broadly consistent though it is with the concept of dialogism, is that it hardly seems related to what Bakhtin himself chooses to do with the idea of genre in his own work. From the moment it appears in the latter's book on Dostoevsky – 'the creator of an essentially new novelistic genre [...] the polyphonic novel' (PDP 7) – genre has been at least as much of a disruptive force as it has been a unifying force in the context of Bakhtin's work as a whole. As we saw in Chapter 7, Bakhtin will later insist that traditional stylistics cannot 'isolate a single definite, stable characteristic of the novel' (EN 8) without immediately destroying that characteristic as a generic marker. Yet his own definition of the novel, which recasts it as uniquely capable of absorbing and dialogizing the languages of heteroglossia, 'a dialogized system made up of the images of "languages", styles and consciousnesses [...]' (PND 49), a 'diversity of social speech types [...] artistically organized' (DN 262), is only tangentially related to the conditions of its 'performance and perception'. In a grand historical narrative of his own, Bakhtin suggests that it is the fact that the novel is 'the only genre younger than writing and the book' (EN 3) that makes it receptive to forces that must somehow elude those genres – once again, lyric, epic and drama – that had acquired their 'finalized' (reified) profile within the literary system of the closed, monoglot world. It is its receptivity to heteroglossia, as we saw in Chapter 7, that makes the novel the only 'genre in a state of becoming' (EN 11), the only genre that 'can comprehend the process of becoming' (EN 7). Its rise to prominence – and here Bakhtin is broadly happy to subscribe to the more conventional narrative of the rise of the novel from the eighteenth century – will increasingly have an impact on the large-scale conditions of performance and perception of other genres, which are fated to become increasingly 'novelized'; but it is hard to square the later sense of the unique capacity and historical pre-eminence of the novel with Medvedev's theory, which purports to account for genre as a total (historical) system. In fact, what 'survives' from Medvedev in Bakhtin's theory of the novel and novelization is the sense in which different genres have different ways of finalizing the material from which they are made; the precise sense in which these different ways of finalizing – seeing, conceptualizing reality – are determined by their actual place in the world is lost.

Bakhtin therefore seems to conceive not of a system of genre, but rather a generic *principle*, which is consistent with his core programme as it evolves from eventness to dialogized heteroglossia, but which threatens, without exaggeration, to *destroy* genre altogether. All 'novels' will be understood as more or less 'novelistic', an increasingly close synonym for 'dialogic' (in fact, Bakhtin makes this simple idea quite explicit in the final section of 'Discourse in the Novel' by organizing the history of the European novel into 'two stylistic lines' (DN 366–415) distinguished by their relationship to dialogized heteroglossia). Eventually, we might project, as 'novelization' has its effect on all other literary genres – when, for example, a 'romantic poem' becomes a 'novelized poem' (EN 7) – that *all* literary works, regardless of even the most profound formal or thematic distinctions between them, will be reduced to the more or less 'novelistic', the more or less profoundly 'dialogic'. Bakhtin has argued that, 'faced with the problem of the novel, genre theory must submit to a radical restructuring' (EN 8), a contention that holds in relation to the seeming unity of epic-lyric-drama, which can find no place for the mixed or hybrid novel form. Yet, Bakhtin's conception of the novel itself threatens also to abolish it as a genre in any meaningful sense: the idea of 'novelness', founded on receptivity to 'becoming' and dialogized heteroglossia, threatens to displace not only the system of genre that has both sustained and struggled with the very idea of the novel, but also the 'novel' itself.

CHRONOTOPE, CARNIVAL AND GENRE

This problem is brought into even sharper focus when we recall that two of the key concepts we have already encountered, chronotope and carnival, can also be viewed specifically as *generic* categories, variations on the theme of 'novelness'. Bakhtin is more insistent on the significance of genre in relation to chronotope than to carnival – 'It can even be said that it is precisely the chronotope that defines genre and generic distinctions' (FTC 84–5) – but both can be seen as ways of defining genre without primary regard for either their surface formal characteristics or their theme, whether or not it is considered in isolation from conditions of performance and perception, the work's place in the world. Works that are generically defined by their chronotope(s) or by the manner in which they embody the 'indestructible' carnival spirit (RW 33) are explicitly differentiated in terms of the different ways in which they finalize the material from which they are made.

This is particularly marked in relation to the chronotope and can be exemplified by approaching chronotopically not 'specific varieties of the novel genre' (FTC 252), as we did in Chapter 8, but rather one of the genres Bakhtin regards as an unprepossessing remnant of the 'closed, monological world' – that same *epic* that Frye has traced back to its roots in song and chant. Bakhtin does not now approach epic explicitly from the point of view of 'performance', but from a differently conceived idea of 'perception'. He pays no attention to its typical formal profile – a narrative composed of lines in dactylic hexameter, or blank or alliterative verse – but does acknowledge the importance of theme: epic is, above all, defined by its orientation towards 'national tradition' and the 'national epic past' (EN 13). The 'epic past' describes more than just the theme of epic, however: it gestures also towards its *chronotope*. The epic is not concerned with the past as such, but conceives of the past in terms of an 'absolute epic distance' (EN 13) which separates the world of the epic from contemporary reality; the epic past is an 'absolute past', 'walled off absolutely from all subsequent times' (EN 15). The term 'epic' can therefore survive the transition from Homer's *Iliad* to the foundational narrative poem in the English vernacular, *Beowulf* (c. 700–1100), or from John Milton's (1608–74) *Paradise Lost* (1667) to Walter Scott's (1771–1832) early romantic *Marmion* (1808). This is not to say that epic does not change, as even these brief examples confirm – the conditions of its performance and perception are constantly changing, including the fact that, with each new variation, the literary context into which it inserts itself changes. But it cannot, while remaining epic, breach the boundary between the present moment of telling (and listening/reading) and the absolute past, which is 'immanent in the form [i.e. the architectonic form] of the epic itself and is felt and heard in its every word' (EN 16):

> To portray an event on the same time-and-value plane as oneself and one's contemporaries (and an event that is therefore based on personal experience and thought) is to step out of the world of the epic into the world of the novel.
>
> (EN 14)

Epic, Bakhtin suggests, cannot survive in the era of the novel, other than as an archaicism, as a parody – or as a *chronotope*, which contributes to a generic profile that is, in sum, other than epic.

Something similar might be said of carnival, which, as we saw in Chapter 9, attaches itself to the 'homeless' minor parodic-travesty-ing forms in 'eras of closed and deaf monoglossia' (EN 12), when the epic, lyric and drama remain self-sufficiently resistant to their influence. Eventually, the 'grotesque image' that is emblematic of carnival finds expression in the non-canonical, boundary-effacing phenomenon that will, from the decisive 'crossroads' moment of Rabelais' *Gargantua and Pantagruel*, transform European literature into something that is successively more and more receptive to the carnivalesque and the grotesque, which become, as we noted in the previous chapter, near synonyms for 'novel'. The (surface) formal profile of a given work is once again close to irrelevant in determining its generic affiliation. Thus, Mikhail Bulgakov's (1891–1940) *Master and Margarita* (1940/1973) is deemed 'carnivalesque', but so too might Angela Carter's (1940–92) *Nights at the Circus* (1984), Irvine Welsh's *Trainspotting* (1993), or Jez Butterworth's (b. 1969) play *Jerusalem* (2009). Just as formal comparison of these works plays little role in their definition as carnivalesque, so too does any reconstruction of their isolated themes – unless the 'carnival spirit' itself is analysed as a 'theme' in Medvedev's sense of 'the organic unity of theme and of what lies beyond it' (FM 133).

Bakhtin's 'novelistic' theory of genre – like Medvedev's, like chronotope, and like carnival, which all but takes us full circle – risks sacrificing genre itself to different manifestations of a core principle; it also fails to accomplish what is quite explicit in Medvedev (and in Voloshinov). Heteroglossia is, after all, primarily a *social* rather than an explicitly literary fact, and Bakhtin intends that his conception of the novel (and other increasingly novelized genres) will realize the task implied by Medvedev's definition of the work as 'a specifically defined socio-historical act' (FM 132) and made more explicit in Voloshinov's earlier definition of genre as a

> *powerful condenser of unspoken social evaluations*: each word in [the literary work] is saturated with them. And these same *social evaluations organize artistic form* as their *unmediated expression*.
>
> (DLDP 76)

Bakhtin's 'dialogic' or 'novelistic' theory of genre is designed, in other words, to marry a theory of literary genre to a translinguistic conception of living language – to do justice to both literature and language beyond literature as fundamentally dialogic phenomena. Yet, this project cannot be completed on the ground of the 'novel' alone, a fact acknowledged by Bakhtin relatively late in his career in the act of returning to the problem of genre for a final time.

SPEECH GENRES AND LITERARY GENRES

Voloshinov summarizes his idea that social evaluation (or psychology) is present in living speech by insisting that it is accessible, specifically,

> in the most varied forms of the 'utterance', in the form of small *speech genres*, inner and outer, which have until this time not been studied at all.
>
> (MPL 20)

Bakhtin himself makes only one fleeting reference to 'speech genres' in his work – at the close of 'From the Prehistory of Novelistic

Discourse' (PND 83) – until in 1952–3, when non-standard research and views on language had once again become possible in the Soviet Union – at which point he returns to them and to the submerged project of translinguistics in search of a different conception of genre.

The key difference, at the simplest of levels, is that genre is here explicitly considered not as a phenomenon restricted to literature, but as something that is both present and significant in all spheres of speech interaction. Literary genres, which have been studied principally in terms of how they differ from *other* literary genres, in fact share a 'common *verbal* (linguistic) nature' (PSG 61) with non-literary genres of speech, such as the command or the private letter. These speech genres, more clearly than their literary counterparts, acquire their stylistic profile from the combination ('organic unity' – Medvedev) of their thematic orientation towards their object and the immediate conditions in which they are produced. All verbal production, literary and non-literary, notwithstanding its 'extreme diversity' (PSG 61), can therefore be studied within a single conceptual and methodological framework. Bakhtin here expresses in slightly different terms the same opposition we encountered in Chapter 7 between the demands of 'a normative-centralizing system of a unitary language' (i.e. universality) and 'living heteroglossia' (i.e. diversity) (DN 272). 'The Problem of Speech Genres' proposes to mediate this opposition by *differentiating* types of discourse, rather than by absolutely distinguishing one from the other – by arranging them on a continuous spectrum instead of erecting insurmountable boundaries between them.

In order to preserve this methodological unity, and in rejection of distinctions founded *per se* on the 'novelness' or chronotopicity of a given work/utterance, Bakhtin differentiates speech genres in terms of their social, formal and functional *complexity*: domestic speech or the military command, for example, are termed simple or 'primary' speech genres, while the novel, the drama, all types of scientific discourse, publicistic genres, etc. are complex or 'second-order' speech genres. We should note immediately that the distinction between primary and second-order speech genres does not map seamlessly onto any distinction between literary and non-literary discourse: large areas of non-literary discourse – scientific discourse, for example – are classified as second-order. The distinction in fact turns on the pragmatic conditions in which primary and second-order speech genres emerge:

> Second-order (complex) speech genres [...] arise in conditions of more complex and relatively highly developed and organized cultural interaction, mainly of a written nature: artistic, scientific, sociopolitical, etc.
>
> (PSG 62)

Genres of speech (discourse) are therefore defined in terms of their particular conditions of performance and perception, which also largely determine their thematic orientation in certain cases: the military command, for example, is heavily constrained by its immediate function, the context of discipline and the relationship between the commanding speaker and the commanded listener; but that context also largely determines what it can be 'about' – 'About turn!' is recognizable and comprehensible as a 'command', whereas 'Sing softly!' would not be: it would entirely disrupt the contextual-semantic profile of the 'genre' (although we should note once again that its *form*, on the surface, is unchanged). There is, in other words, no scope whatsoever for 'individual style' in a simple speech genre such as the military command; there is significantly more – albeit still profoundly constrained, as we have seen, by the conventions of the genre – in literary epic; and, perhaps predictably, it is the novel that once again stands at the far end of this spectrum, permitting, if not guaranteeing, *maximal* freedom – novels can be 'about' anything at all and are designed to allow the incorporation and dialogization of the full diversity of speech types. The novel is, we might say, the second-order speech genre *par excellence*.

The complexity of speech genres is not, however, simply a matter of individual style, nor even of the complexity of *immediate* conditions of performance and perception. This is because

> in the process of their formation [second-order speech genres] absorb into themselves and rework various primary (simple) genres, which arose in conditions of direct verbal interaction. These primary genres, on entering into the structure of the complex, are transformed and acquire a particular character: they lose their direct relation to actual reality and to the real utterances of others. Domestic dialogue or letters in a novel, for example, while preserving their form and everyday meaning only on the plane

> of the content of the novel, enter into actual reality only through the novel
> as a whole, that is as a literary-artistic event and not one of everyday life.
>
> (PSG 62)

The complex, second-order genres are quite literally made out of the simple, primary genres – the private letter, the military command, different types of everyday conversation. These are recontextualized in the context of a literary work – a novel, for example – retaining their stylistic profile at an immediate level, but becoming a (dialogic) element in a larger stylistic profile, that of the work as a whole. The fundamental relationship in any consideration of genre becomes the relationship between second-order genres and the primary or simple genres, which are transformatively incorporated into the second-order, complex genres. Primary genres are indeed formed in the course of direct, actual interaction between people and social groups across the full range of human contact and are then 'reused' in formation of the second-order genres; the second-order genres are formed in the course of a different kind of social interaction, a higher-level, more complex kind, which might involve interaction between commercial enterprises (publishers), institutions of criticism, indeed the entire social, cultural and economic environment in which literary schools, trends and indeed genres form themselves. Bakhtin had written in the 1930s, in expression of the force with which the concept of genre had first entered his work, that genres were nothing less than the *heroes* of literary history:

> Beneath the superficial hustle and bustle of literary process [are] the
> major and crucial fates of literature and language, whose great heroes
> turn out to be first and foremost genres, and whose 'trends' and 'schools'
> are but second- or third-rank protagonists.
>
> (EN 8)

Now in the 1950s, in Bakhtin's only attempt at an extensive synthesis of his and his colleagues' earlier work, genres take on a yet more 'heroic' role: first, speech genres provide a way to theorize what literature is and what it is not – to theorize how literature does not transcend other types of verbal activity, but is in fact closely related to and derives from them. Second, the second-order genres not only take advantage of the 'ready-made' form of the primary genres, incorporating and transforming them in order to produce something more 'complex', but in so doing, they also lay bare entire processes of sociolinguistic evolution. Genres are not only the 'heroes' of literary history, but of the historical relationship between literature and society. Historical changes in literature are related to historical changes in social relations through the specific mechanism of genre. To return to terms we encountered in Chapters 3 and 4 in consideration of the early 'philosophical' Bakhtin, the relationship between 'art' and 'life', in all its microcosmic detail and macrocosmic range, becomes not only perceptible, but perceptible in a state of change ('becoming') in genres, literary and otherwise:

> In order to understand the complex historical dynamic of [the stylistic systems of literary and non-literary language], in order to progress from the simple (and in most cases superficial) description of the styles which are present, and which replace one another, to a historical explanation of these changes, it is necessary to accomplish a particularly orientated examination of the history of speech genres (and not only the second-order, but also the primary). Speech genres more directly, clearly and flexibly reflect all the changes that take place in the life of a society. Utterances and their types, that is, speech genres are the drive belts between the history of society and the history of language.
>
> (PSG 65)

SUMMARY

Genre, at first glance a definitively literary category, begins to influence Bakhtin's work after its theorization in Medvedev's *The Formal Method in Literary Scholarship: A Critical Introduction to Sociological Poetics*, which rejects a mechanistic theory of genre built around the Formalist concept of the device. Many of Bakhtin's key ideas – novelness, the chronotope, carnival – can be seen as variations on the theme of genre; but it is in his late attempt to synthesize genre and Voloshinov's translinguistics that it acquires a central significance for Bakhtin's work as a whole. Speech genres provide a frame in which the idea of literature as a 'condenser of social evaluations' can be traced in practical terms, in the process establishing literary forms as part of a continuous spectrum of verbal production, cognate with, but generically distinguished from, other types of speech and writing. Genre is therefore the category in which the variously (trans)linguistic, literary, and social strands of Bakhtin's work cohere into what is as close to a 'unified' theory as he produced at any stage of his life. Genre emerges as a category that is at once literary and 'trans-literary', and, as we will see in the following chapter, it also has particular significance for Bakhtin's conception of the Humanities.

11

AFTER BAKHTIN

It is intrinsically difficult to assess the impact of any thinker. The task of reflecting on what pertains 'after' the fact of someone's life and writings invites the risk of casting that person as the simple 'cause' of an identifiable 'effect'. These terms, and the implied relationship between them, should always be treated with caution, but this is particularly so in relation to Bakhtin. As we saw at the outset, Bakhtin's life was a discontinuous affair, the process of publication and translation of his work deeply fragmented. This has meant that Bakhtin has sometimes benefited from changes in the critical context between the time of writing and the time of publication of certain works and that he has sometimes even indirectly affected the context of his own reception. When we reflect also on the idea that remains a constant, if necessarily changing, presence throughout Bakhtin's work – the dialogic as 'an almost universal phenomenon, permeating all human speech and all relationships and manifestations of human life, everything that has meaning and significance' (PDP 40) – discussion of 'influence' becomes extremely problematic, if not in fact entirely meaningless. The problem of 'influence' itself can be subsumed in the universality of the dialogic:

> Two juxtaposed utterances belonging to different people who know
> nothing about one another if they only slightly converge on one and the

same subject (idea), inevitably enter into dialogic relations with one another. They come into contact with one another on the territory of a common theme, a common idea.

(PT 114–5)

From agreement to outright rejection, and at all points in between, words spoken (written) on a related theme – 'the word encountering its object' (DN 276) – *always* enter into dialogical relations. Bakhtin's work therefore requires to be read in dialogue with any and every one of its many potential points of intersection, which will vary with each and every reader of this book. Rather than focus too slavishly on a putative 'legacy', this chapter will therefore suggest some of its own 'points of intersection' and assess how Bakhtin can be mobilized as a productive force in relation to them.

One dramatic example of the dangers of confusing influence and consanguinity is the way sociolinguistics has emerged and developed in the second half of the twentieth century to the point where, by the time Bakhtin's and Voloshinov's theory of discourse had found an audience outside Russia, it already appeared 'domesticated', broadly consistent with the modern sense of language as a social and performative phenomenon that had been pursued by various branches of sociolinguistics. A specific example might be the apparent similarities between the Bakhtinian theory of the utterance and what became known as 'speech act theory'. John L. Austin's (1911–60) *How to do Things with Words* (1962) introduced the idea that speaking is often also a *performance* of something, an action, as much a kind of 'doing' as physical action: to promise that you will do something is as much an 'action' as the act you will later perform, for example. Speech act theory is an element of a broader area of linguistics known as pragmatics, which belatedly explores the social capacity of language identified but largely ignored by Saussure, investigating how context ('conditions of performance and perception', perhaps) is constitutive of the significance of what is said – every bit as important as the 'abstract' rules of grammar or word formation. Pragmatics in general and speech act theory in particular seem to resonate with elements of Bakhtin's and Voloshinov's translinguistics; they might even be said to have assisted Bakhtin's and Voloshinov's belated reception – while at the same time effacing some of the specifics of Bakhtin's thought. Speech is *always* an act for Bakhtin, regardless of its intentionality or the 'type' of speech act being performed, for example; and an 'act', which is ethically undersigned by the person performing it, is not the same as an 'action', which is a purely neutral descriptive category; also, and as we have seen, 'context' cannot be thought of in isolation from the architectonic relationships of the subjects present in that context.

From a different perspective, the development of modern poetry, its embrace of speech diversity and the centrality of, precisely, voice, has made Bakhtin's preference for the novel over verse seem doctrinaire and almost cruel – although Bakhtin would perhaps counter that this is only further proof of the ongoing 'novelization' of poetry and all other non-novelistic modes, which have become infected with the novel's 'spirit of becoming and unfinalizability' (EN 7), eventually brought into the gravitational field of 'the reality of heteroglossia' (DN 271). Even literature itself begins to look, after Bakhtin, more Bakhtinian, but once again without the implication of any simple relationship of cause and effect. What has caught up with or overhauled Bakhtin, undermined or vindicated him, further problematizes already difficult questions of reception and influence.

Despite these caveats, there is no doubt that Bakhtin retains enormous potential not just for literary studies, but also for the Humanities in general. The question of his impact on the wider world beyond literature and the Humanities and his potentiality in that context is more complex – as complex, in fact, as Bakhtin's conception of the relationship between art and life that we examined in Chapters 3 and 4, which remains a live but less explicit force throughout his later work. This chapter will therefore assess Bakhtin's impact and utility under these two successive headings, namely literary studies and the Humanities, before offering a 'last word' about the world 'beyond' both literature and the Humanities.

LITERARY STUDIES AFTER BAKHTIN

Michael Holquist has suggested that Bakhtin casts received understanding of intellectual history in a 'weird light' (Bakhtin 1981: xvii); the same might be said, with even greater force, of his impact on literary studies. The sense of 'weird' here is close to the meaning of 'uncanny', whereby apparently familiar literary properties – form, irony, intertextuality and realism, for example – seem to retain the characteristics that make them identifiable, but are at the same time forever changed. A strangeness is cast over the familiar, while what is strange becomes disturbing not because it is strange, but because it takes on an appearance of uneasy familiarity. Bakhtin does not negate or destroy familiar literary categories, which retain at least their outward appearance, but which, at the same time, acquire a deeper value and significance.

Irony, for example, is both undermined and renewed when considered in the context of double-voiced discourse and the dialogic. Conventionally, the various species of irony are defined in terms of a distance or contradiction between what is said, seen or supposed and what the reader or audience are invited to understand. Whether in dramatic irony, where the audience might understand that a given character's actions are contrary to his or her best interests – where the audience, basically, knows more than the character – or in verbal irony, where what is intended does not equate to what is literally stated, the emphasis is not on the situations or meanings in themselves, but rather on the space between them – on the fact, constitutive of irony, of their non-coincidence. In Bakhtinian terms, irony remains an empty, 'abstract' category until such non-coincidence is explicitly *personalized*: the relationship between what is said, what is understood by the character to whom it is said, and what is understood by the reader must be viewed in terms of the concrete architectonics of the event of encounter between embodied subjects. It is not distance or non-coincidence as such that matters, but rather the specific mechanics of the relationship between those 'persons' who encounter one another across that distance – which, consistent with the constitutive power of outsideness in the process of 'forming', is a precondition for, but not the definitive essence of, any 'irony'. As we saw in examples from *Little Dorrit* and *Bleak House* in Chapter 7, light comic irony, which might otherwise remain a somewhat two-dimensional phenomenon, reflected in a relationship that is established between author and reader at the 'hero's' *expense*, becomes multidimensional when imbricated in the architectonic structure of the event of the encounter between many consciousnesses – when it is embodied and becomes part of the structure of the event. Bakhtin will even argue late in life that there can be no speech or writing *without* irony, because all discourse, whether intentionally or otherwise, is conditioned by the distance of the double-voiced: 'Irony is everywhere [...]. Modern man does not proclaim; he speaks. That is, he speaks with reservations' (N70 132). Irony, too, as a manifestation of double-voiced discourse, becomes a near synonym for the dialogic.

Something similar might be said of the foundational literary category of form, as indeed we began to see in Chapter 4 in discussing architectonics. Form for Bakhtin is not *primarily* a question of what he regards as surface or compositional characteristics, from iambic pentameter to blank verse to third-person narration. These are all significant in the literary work not in themselves, but in terms of the function they perform in relation to the architectonics of the event(s) of the interior world of a given literary world and to the interlocking (and overarching) architectonics of the 'event' of the literary work itself. Form is a function of the dialogic relations between author, hero and reader. Two works that are superficially similar in terms of their surface, compositional formal profile may be worlds apart in terms of their deep, architectonic formal profile. Just as we earlier (Chapter 7) insisted that comparing Hugo's *Les Misérables* to Camus' *L'Étranger* on any formal or stylistic basis would be absurd (notwithstanding that they are both 'novels'), it would be equally misleading to assert that marked formal and stylistic similarities between *Les Misérables* and Dumas' (1802–70) *Le Comte de Monte-Cristo* (1844–45) are as significant as the deep architectonic (and chronotopic) distinctions between the two novels.

Even a term such as 'intertextuality', which conventionally denotes the definitive interrelatedness of literary texts – which is opposed, in other words, to any conception of the literary text as self-enclosed – appears to be simultaneously supported and undermined in Bakhtin. An intertextual reading of any given text might seek to establish the other texts that are 'present' within it and thereby establish that the production of meaning relies not on the one-dimensional inscription of authorial intention in *this* text, but rather upon the inter-animation of many texts, not all of which are, clearly, under the 'control' of a single author. Intertextuality would appear, therefore, to imply a 'dialogic' relationship between texts, the necessary imbrication of a given text in (potentially) the entire history of prior literary production. To take a very basic example, which casts a different light on our invocation of Brontë's *Jane Eyre* in relation to the chronotope in Chapter 8, the meaning and effect of Jean Rhys' (1890–1979) *Wide Sargasso Sea* (1966), which reconstructs part of the past of both Rochester and Bertha, is made implicitly dependent on an intertextual relationship with the earlier work (and, more powerfully, the meaning of *Jane Eyre* is potentially transformed by its intertextual relationship with the later work). For Bakhtin, however, this is once again a 'surface' relationship, however compelling and even indispensable it might appear to be for a reading of *Jane Eyre* and/or *Wide Sargasso Sea*. Bakhtin's description of the mechanics of universal dialogism (which we encountered in Chapter 6 and again at the beginning of this chapter in discussion of Bakhtin's own 'influence') insists that *any* utterance (including the literary work)

> finds the object towards which it is directed always and already qualified, as it were, disputed, evaluated, enveloped by an obscuring mist, or, on the contrary, by the light of other words already spoken about it.
>
> (DN 276)

The 'universality' of dialogic relations therefore universalizes the possibility of intertextual (or inter-speech) relations. It is important not just to establish relations between particular texts on an isolated thematic basis, but also to be aware that *all* living discourse, literary or otherwise, enters the 'dialogically agitated and tension-filled environment of other words, evaluations and accents' (DN 276) and that the implied subject positions or social evaluations that determine this environment are therefore somehow 'present' in the text under discussion, determining its semantic and stylistic profile. For Bakhtin, *all* textuality is intertextuality; but the identification of intertextuality without a definitive focus on underlying dialogic relations is as empty as any theory of the self-enclosed and self-sufficient text it seeks to displace.

On another level, if we evoke the more conventional large-scale literary-historical categories such as sentimentalism or realism, related effects can be observed. Bakhtin does not seek to deconstruct realism, for example, by explicitly undermining the mimetic principle that stands at its heart or by exposing the conventions that have been developed to maintain the illusion of equivalence between the text and 'reality'. He argues instead that the equivalences implied by mimesis must also be understood as dialogic equivalences and that the very conventions that support such equivalences are, like 'compositional form', close to meaningless when considered in isolation from the embodied subjects of – and beyond – the fictional world. Thus, Dostoevsky's realism consists in its sophisticated staging of encounters between 'living subjects': it is a realism 'in the highest sense', consistent with Bakhtin's approving citation of Dostoevsky's own self-assessment: "'They call me a *psychologist*. This is not true; I am [...] a realist *in the highest sense* [...]'" (PDP 60). This Bakhtinian (Dostoevskian) realism is adequate not just to surface appearances, however complex, but to all verbalized human interaction, in all its dialogic, unfinalizable eventness; it is, like everything in Bakhtin, an emblem or component of an overarching and explicitly *ethical* aesthetic built around the body, person and speech of the human subject – around '*expressive* and *speaking* being'.

The novel or 'novelness', as we have seen, has come to stand for this aesthetic more than any other phenomenon – thus casting the novel itself in the 'weird light' that in fact transforms and preserves all literary categories. The novel, as we have also seen, becomes a limit point for the sustainability of any conventional theory of genre – but also, paradoxically, for the repeated attempts Bakhtin and his colleagues have made to recast and reinvigorate genre. Here, however, it is not only genre that begins to appear in a weird light; Bakhtin's final theorization of genre, outlined in the previous chapter, makes explicit a productive theoretical concern that has been quietly present in his work from the beginning – a concern about where *literature* itself begins and ends.

THE HUMANITIES AFTER BAKHTIN: GENRE AND DISCIPLINE

It is tempting to approach the question of Bakhtin and the Humanities across the particular territory through which literary studies has interfaced with the other Human Sciences over the period in which Bakhtin has come to prominence – literary and critical theory. This particular area of a broader intellectual history does indeed appear in a 'weird light' after Bakhtin, who places the all-too persistent opposition between theory and Humanism under a profound question mark. There is, however, a more direct route from literature to the Humanities broadly conceived, which proceeds from the 'expressive and speaking being' referred to above, as well as from the now no longer exclusively literary category of *genre*.

'Expressive and speaking being' is precisely how Bakhtin defines 'the object of the human sciences'. This is intended, first, to distinguish Human Sciences from the Natural Sciences: in the late essay 'The Problem of the Text in Linguistics, Philology, and the Human Sciences: An Experiment in Philosophical Analysis', and in a reprise of the critique of theoreticism we encountered in Chapter 3, Bakhtin characterizes the object of the Natural Sciences in terms of its *givenness*: it is 'given as a thing' (PT 106). It does not, like the object of the Human Sciences, have a *voice*, it does not speak back to the observer or researcher. Understanding in the Humanities is a 'reflection of a reflection' (PT 113), in which 'research becomes inquiry and conversation, that is, dialogue', whereas in the Natural Sciences, 'we do not address inquiries to nature and she does not answer us' (PT 114). There can be no dialogic relationship with the object of the Natural Sciences, but in the Humanities 'understanding is always dialogic to some degree' (PT 111). The relevant criterion in the Humanities is 'depth of understanding' (PT 127), as opposed to the series of slightly pejorative terms Bakhtin uses to emphasize the 'exactness' of the exact (natural) sciences: 'transcription', 'duplication', 'precision', etc.:

> The exact sciences are a monological form of knowledge [...] Here there is only one subject, the subject that knows (contemplates) and speaks (utters). There stands before [this subject] only a *voiceless thing*. Any object can be received and cognized as a thing. But the subject as such cannot be received or studied as a thing, because, as a subject, it cannot become voiceless and remain a subject; consequently, cognition of [the subject] can only be *dialogical*.

> (TMHS 161)

Once again, in line with the core idea of the 'once-occurrent event of being', which we discussed in Chapter 3, understanding in the

Humanities 'is never a tautology or duplication' (PT 115), because in fact understanding *creates* something new in the consciousness of the understanding subject. There are 'given' elements in the object of Humanities disciplines – language, for example, conceived as an abstract system – but focusing on the given at the expense of *what is created* is to reduce the Humanities also to a *monological* form of knowledge.

On another level, 'expressive and speaking being' allows Bakhtin to establish a common basis for the Humanities disciplines themselves:

> The text (written and oral) is the primary given of all these disciplines and of all thought in the human sciences [...]. The text is the unmediated reality (a reality of thought and experience) from which these disciplines and this thought can emerge. Where there is no text, there is no object of study or of thought.
>
> (PT 103)

If thought in the Humanities is definitively 'directed towards other thoughts, ideas, meanings' and these are 'realized and made available to the researcher only in the form of a *text*', then the text itself is 'the only possible point of departure [...] regardless of the goals of the research' (PT 104).

It is notable in this connection that, although he does not embark on a series of distinctions within the Humanities, Bakhtin does raise the same problem we encountered in the previous chapter, namely 'the problem of the functions of the text' and what he now calls '*textual* genres' (PT 104, my emphasis). In fact, there is no difference between 'speech genres' and 'textual genres', as 'text' explicitly covers what is said as well as what is written. So the 'texts' that are the object of Humanities disciplines might take the form of speech samples in sociolinguistics, oral testimony in history, poems and novels in literary studies, political writings in political science, for example; and these texts, as we have seen, can be approached from the point of view of Bakhtin's speech-genres model in ways that acknowledge their commonality as phenomena between which there can be dialogic relations, and that at the same time identify their functional and stylistic specificity as 'types' of utterance, with their own contexts or 'conditions of performance and perception' and typical thematic concerns. Their 'common verbal nature' is established on a level of significant generality; their varying but identifiable style and function is established on a level of equally significant particularity.

We have seen how a 'second-order' genre such as the novel incorporates and transforms primary genres that are formed in the course of direct, actual interaction between people and social groups across the full range of human contact – which on the level of the primary may in fact resemble very closely the range of 'speech samples' we identified as a potential object for socio-linguistics. The 'form and everyday meaning' (PSG 62) of such speech might be identical, its stylistic and semantic profile unchanged; but both its function and the way in which it enters into 'actual reality' are entirely different in each case – it becomes architecto-nically determined by its generic location. Further, some novels, such as Günter Grass' (b. 1927) *The Tin Drum* (1959), might incorporate a more stylistically and functionally developed speech genre that resembles the oral testimony we identified as a potential object for history. In all three cases, different genres do different things with the 'same' material, which is transformed as it is incorporated into its new generic location. The speech-genres model offers a way of beginning, in quite practical terms, to iden-tify the generic – and therefore social and historical – relations between literary genres and 'not literature'.

In addition to the 'not literature' of the everyday genres, how-ever, 'not literature' possesses another, quite particular territory. When we consider that 'textual genres' might also take the form of essays, articles and books in sociolinguistics, literary studies, his-tory and political science, the speech-genres model becomes a way of identifying also the 'generic' – and therefore, potentially at least, social and historical – relations between *disciplines* in the Huma-nities and beyond. Thinking about disciplines, more or less, as genres, with their own conditions of performance and perception and their own ways of orientating themselves towards their 'sub-ject matter' is what takes Bakhtin's reflection on the similarities and differences between disciplines beyond the simple contention that the dialogic 'method' – although it is always more (and indeed less) than a 'method' – is not only relevant to but *necessary for* any discipline for which text and speech are 'the primary given', from sociolinguistics to philosophy, from literary studies to history, from anthropology to political science. Just like genres, their 'common nature' is established on a level of significant generality; their varying, but identifiable style and function is established on a level of equally significant particularity.

Texts are the primary given for Humanities disciplines in two or more senses, as we have seen: 'primary' (everyday speech, oral testimony, etc.) and the different variants of 'second-order' (novels, critical essays about novels, historiography, etc.). Yet the text is also, to modify this terminology, a 'secondary given' for the scientific disciplines; even the scientific disciplines, the objects of which 'don't speak', and between which there can therefore be no dialogic relations, must themselves 'speak' through the text. 'Scientific discourse' is also a cluster of second-order genres of speech, susceptible on a secondary level to the 'reality of heteroglossia' and the universal influence of dialogism; but these forces will not act upon and determine the profile of such discourse in as profound a manner as is the case, at different extremes, with everyday speech or with novels. This allows Bakhtin to insist, on one hand, on a 'strict demarcation between understanding and scientific study', while on the other maintaining that there is no 'insurmountable barrier' between the Human and Natural Sciences (N70 145). They represent different forms of knowledge, which can be related to one another only according to a 'strict demarcation', before being differentiated in terms of the 'textual genres' they generate. Just as the Humanities can be reduced to a monological form of knowledge, so too can – must – the *necessarily* monological form of knowledge that is science be dialogized, not in relation to its primary object (a strictly subject-object relationship), but on a secondary level as it generates utterances and types of utterance on its range of themes – as it is communicated by and to (other) subjects.

Language – or rather discourse – turns out to be what we called at the outset 'the high road of interdisciplinarity' in profoundly inclusive ways, the site on which Bakhtin proposes to theorize the Humanities in ways that make explicit (and thus protect) an understanding both of their fundamental condition and of their *differentia specifica*. It is also the site on which he proposes to 'demarcate' the Humanities from other forms of knowledge, thus making possible a 'dialogue' between them that will not be conducted on the basis of the primary monologism of scientific discourse. Bakhtin implies that the practice of interdisciplinarity will remain what the French literary and cultural theorist Roland Barthes (1915–80) called a 'pious wish' (Barthes 1977: 155) until the advent of what we might call a 'polyglossia of the disciplines', a distant analogy of the polyglossia Bakhtin has identified as changing linguistic consciousness itself (Chapter 7); instead, however, of languages and cultures inter-animating one another, becoming in the process 'something entirely different', disciplines themselves must enter a parallel 'open Galilean world' of many disciplines, 'mutually animating each other' (PND 61). The Humanities after Bakhtin will be a form of study that 'move[s] in the liminal spheres, that is, on the borders of all the aforementioned disciplines, at their junctures and points of intersection' (PT 103), a world of 'benevolent demarcation. Without border disputes. Cooperation' (N70 137). Bakhtin has felt the need to emphasize 'strict demarcation', but manifestly prefers 'benevolent demarcation and *only then* cooperation' (N70 136, my emphasis). No expression better sums him up.

LAST WORDS: THE WORLD BEYOND THE HUMANITIES

This discussion of disciplines, their place in the Humanities, and the Humanities' relationship to other forms of knowledge shows once again the persistence in Bakhtin's thought of questions of 'worlds' and the imagined or real 'boundaries' between them. Monologic discourse is 'one-sided, bounded, incapable of exhausting its object' (PND 55); epic as a genre is shut off from the contemporary moment of its readership by a 'boundary [that] is immanent in the form of the epic itself' (EN 16). Yet this focus on boundaries is evidence, once again, of how Bakhtin is willing to utilize a term and at the same time efface or change its meaning. Boundaries, as such, only exist in his thought in order for their status as boundaries to be undermined: 'the cultural domain has no inner territory: it is entirely located on boundaries, and boundaries intersect its every element […]' (PCMF 274). Everything is most dialogically alive for Bakhtin 'on the boundary between its own context and another, alien context' (DN 284). Even science, as we have seen above, needs to be (benevolently) demarcated, but does not exist on the far side of some 'insurmountable barrier'. This pertains most spectacularly, as we have seen, to the human body, which is specifically 'the unfinished and open body', which 'is not separated from the world by clearly defined boundaries; it is blended with the world' (RW 26–7). Speech, literary works, literary genres, academic disciplines, even bodies are most alive, at their most productive, when conceived of in terms of dialogical transgression, when they reveal that the provisional boundaries that help structure our idea of them are in fact illusory. Dialogical thought is fundamentally a work of sublation.

This bears directly on what is the most persistent of all 'boundaries' in Bakhtin, which is expressed in terms of 'art' and 'life' in his earlier works, and which settles to the more inclusive, and indeed exhaustive, 'culture' and 'life' by the end of his career: first, 'literature is an inseparable part of culture and it cannot be understood outside the total context of the entire culture of a given epoch' (RQ 2); second, and decisively, 'the world of culture and literature is essentially as boundless as the universe' (N70 140) – as 'boundless' as Voloshinov's earlier description of the 'ocean of inner speech' (MPL 85). Bakhtin's determination to break out from 'the immanent circle of literary studies' that we observed in Chapter 7, the desire to connect it with 'other worlds', appears ultimately as a relatively 'weak' statement of his theoretical programme, which in fact exposes any hard and fast boundaries between one 'world' and another as entirely illusory. Literature/culture and 'life', 'the world' or 'society', we might say, are *co-present*, imbricated in one another, 'unthinkable' in isolation – but at the same time are not simply the 'same': they do not 'duplicate' or 'transcribe' one another, they cannot be reduced to one another.

This is more than a purely 'theoretical' point; in fact, it has profound 'practical' significance (assuming of course that the putative boundary between 'theory' and 'practice' dissolves under a Bakhtinian light). The inseparability of literature, culture (and academic thought), on one hand, and the 'life world' that is no longer 'beyond' it, but it fact contains it, on the other, is the context for a Bakhtin who has been somewhat neglected in the English-speaking world. This is a Bakhtin for whom the 'real' object of research in the Humanities is 'social (public) man' (PT 113), for whom the purpose and function of dialogic thinking is to reveal the discursively encoded boundaries that permit the construction of gender, ethnicity and social class. Dialogic thought and the categories it produces, although they are, as we have seen, intimately related to literature, are not in any sense limited either to literature or culture in its conventional sense. 'Culture' in the Bakhtinian sense is all too literally 'boundless', extending, like dialogic relations, into 'all human speech and all relationships and manifestations of human life, everything that has meaning and significance' (PDP 40). 'Culture' and 'discourse' (the word) combine in Bakhtin to equate to something very much like ideology, relieved of all the 'abstract', 'theoreticist', 'de-personalized' baggage with which it has been burdened, the proper object not of a sociological or 'philosophical' inquiry, but of the distinctive blend of aesthetics and ethics whose name is dialogics.

This process of 'studying' culture/discourse/ideology in dialogic relations, like the dialogic process itself, is also 'boundless'; it has no end, because

> The word wants to be heard, understood, responded to, and again to respond to the response, and so forth *ad infinitum*. It enters into a dialogue that does not have a semantic end [...].
>
> (PT 127)

Dialogic thought implies an orientation not towards 'necessity', but rather towards 'possibility' (N70 139), towards an immediate future context that is no less concrete than the present:

> The anticipated context of the future: a sense that I am taking a new step (have progressed). Stages in the dialogic movement of *understanding*: the point of departure, the given text; movement backward, past contexts; movement forward, anticipation (and the beginning) of a future context.
>
> (TMHS 161–2)

Bakhtin's own last words emphasize, above all, that there can be no 'end' to the 'dialogic movement', that it is both expressive and constitutive of unfinalizability:

> There is neither a first nor a last word and there are no limits to the dialogic context (it extends into the boundless past and the boundless future). Even past meanings, that is, those born in the dialogue of past

centuries, can never be stable (finalized, ended once and for all) – they will always change (be renewed) in the process of subsequent future development of the dialogue. At any moment in the development of the dialogue there are immense, boundless masses of forgotten contextual meanings, but at certain moments of the dialogue's subsequent development along the way they are recalled and invigorated in renewed form (in a new context). Nothing is absolutely dead: every meaning will have its homecoming festival.

(TMHS 170)

Homecoming festival? Boundless masses ...

FURTHER READING

This section is structured in three parts, each one offering a different way to follow up on the arguments contained in this book:

- Part 1 covers the English-language editions of Bakhtin (and Voloshinov and Medvedev), with brief commentary on publication details and on contents (details of individual essays contained in many of these editions are given in the 'Abbreviations' section at the beginning of this book).
- Part 2 gives full references for other works cited, covering both literary exemplars and specific theoretical or philosophical texts.
- Part 3 focuses on selected book-length studies and edited collections on Bakhtin written in (or translated into) English. In view of the sheer volume of material that has been published on Bakhtin over the past thirty years, and in view also of the relative accessibility of the work by Bakhtin himself, this section is deliberately brief. It also makes no attempt to imply a particular 'canonical' perspective on Bakhtin, but rather to direct the reader towards a broadly representative set of sources, which might form a useful interpretive context for engagement with the materials in Part 1.

1. PRIMARY SOURCES

BAKHTIN

Rabelais and His World, trans. Hélène Iswolsky (Bloomington: Indiana University Press, 1968).

The work through which Bakhtin was first introduced to the English-speaking world, thereby establishing carnival, the grotesque, and folk laughter at the heart of perceptions of Bakhtin in the West, associations which have persisted through the many changes of emphasis in subsequently translated work. The original began as Bakhtin's doctoral dissertation and was written and rewritten over a period of twenty-five years before belated publication in the Soviet Union in 1965. The pioneering nature of the translation now seems undermined by numerous misprisions and omissions; partly because of this, what was once Bakhtin's best-known work perhaps remains his most commonly misunderstood.

The Dialogic Imagination: Four Essays by M.M. Bakhtin, ed. Michael Holquist, trans. Caryl Emerson and Michael Holquist (University of Texas Press Slavic Series No. 1) (Austin: University of Texas Press, 1981).

Contains the key extended essay 'Discourse in the Novel', alongside 'Epic and Novel', 'From the Prehistory of Novelistic Discourse', and 'Forms of Time and of the Chronotope in the Novel', all of which were written in the 1930s and published in Russian only in 1975. The collection as a whole is slightly deceptive in its implication of the related status of its components, which, although all ostensibly concerned with the novel, are in many ways distinct in the conception of the novelistic they present. 'Discourse in the Novel' is one of Bakhtin's most important works, his most concentrated treatment of the idea of dialogism in literature.

Problems of Dostoevsky's Poetics, ed. and trans. Caryl Emerson (Minneapolis and London: University of Minnesota Press, 1984).

Unique in Bakhtin's oeuvre, in that the original version was published in Russian under Bakhtin's own name close to the time of its completion (1929), albeit at a moment when its author was under house arrest. The book was begun in the early part of the decade, its second part written much later, under the ambivalent influence of Russian Formalism, of which it offers a dialogic critique; the book therefore forms an instructive bridge between the early 'philosophical' Bakhtin and his later, more explicit focus on the literary. The 1929 publication was entitled 'Problems of Dostoevsky's *Art*', while the 1963 edition, featuring an entirely new chapter on the carnivalesque and Mennipean satire, became 'Problems of Dostoevsky's *Poetics*' – and becomes even more of a hybrid than it was in 1929.

Speech Genres and other Late Essays, ed. Caryl Emerson and Michael Holquist, trans. Vern W. McGee (University of Texas Press Slavic Series No. 8) (Austin: University of Texas Press, 1986).

The most varied of the English-language collections of Bakhtin; it includes 'The Problem of Speech Genres' (written in 1952–3), the surviving fragment of the work on the *Bildungsroman*, which dates from the late 1930s and bears largely on the problem of the chronotope, as well as a number of later essays and fragments, including 'The Problem of the Text' and 'Toward a Methodology for the Human Sciences', which are indispensable for an understanding of Bakhtin's importance for the Humanities in general. The varied nature of the material has, however, led to a number of problems with the translations, which are slightly less surefooted than both earlier and later Texas Slavic editions.

Art and Answerability: Early Philosophical Essays by M.M. Bakhtin, ed. Michael Holquist and Vadim Liapunov, trans. Vadim Liapunov and Kenneth Brostrom (University of Texas Press Slavic Series No. 9) (Austin: University of Texas Press, 1990).

This volume might easily have been entitled 'Author and Hero in Aesthetic Activity', after the long (and unfinished) essay from the early 1920s that forms its main part and which sets out the core of Bakhtin's aesthetic programme. It also contains the early short

statement 'Art and Answerability' (1919) and Bakhtin's philosophical 'response' to Formalism, 'The Problem of Content, Material, and Form in Verbal Art' (written in 1924 and published in
1979).

Toward a Philosophy of the Act, ed. Vadim Liapunov and
Michael Holquist, trans. Vadim Liapunov (University of Texas
Press Slavic Series No. 10) (Austin: University of Texas Press,
1993).

Bakhtin's first extended work, written c. 1921 and published in
1986, which contains the first elucidation of the concepts of eventness, answerability, outsideness and unfinalizability that form the
basic infrastructure of his thought. Like 'Author and Hero in Aesthetic Activity', this work is incomplete; it is also the only surviving
work to be written, in part, in a technical, philosophical idiom,
which presents certain difficulties for the contemporary reader.

VOLOSHINOV

Freudianism: A Marxist Critique, ed. and trans. I.R. Titunik
(with Neal H. Bruss) (New York: Academic Press, 1976).
[Reprinted in Verso's 'Radical Thinkers' series in 2013].

Published in Russian in 1927, this is a polemical repudiation of the
basis of Freud's thought, ostensibly written for a 'popular' audience.
Later the subject of a controversy over its authorship, the book's
main target is the Freudian conception of the unconscious, which is
dismissed as a 'fiction'. Voloshinov's alternative is the beginnings
of a theory of language as a profoundly and fundamentally social
phenomenon. Also contains a translation of 'Discourse in Life and
Discourse in Poetry'.

Marxism and the Philosophy of Language, trans. Ladislav
Matejka and I.R. Titunik (Cambridge and London: Harvard
University Press, 1986 [1973]).

Published in 1929, this is the most important of the various works
later controversially attributed to Bakhtin, but not published under

his name. The title is somewhat misleading, in that Voloshinov's theories of the utterance and the sign, and of consciousness and the social are attempts to outline a sophisticated materialist 'philosophy of language', as opposed to something that could be described narrowly as 'Marxist'. The book is closely related to the structure of Bakhtin's early thought and at the same time introduces a significant innovation – an explicit focus on the workings of language (discourse) that forms the basis of a Bakhtinian 'translinguistics' and conditions the direction of much of Bakhtin's later thinking.

MEDVEDEV

The Formal Method in Literary Scholarship: A Critical Introduction to Sociological Poetics, trans. Albert J. Wehrle (Baltimore: Johns Hopkins University Press, 1978).

Originally published in 1928, this, as its title suggests, is ostensibly a critique of Russian Formalism, which polemically focuses largely on the Formalists' earlier work. It also introduces the concept of genre into the work of the Bakhtin Circle, as well as providing a survey of how Bakhtinian positions impact on a range of issues central to literary study – language, form and history.

2. OTHER WORKS CITED

Anon. *Beowulf* (University of Exeter, 1988). [c. 700–1100 A.D.]

Apuleius. *The Golden Ass* (Penguin, 1998). [c. 125–180 A.D.]

Austin, John L. *How to do Things with Words* (Clarendon Press, 1962).

Barthes, Roland. *Image-Music-Text*, trans. Stephen Heath (Fontana, 1977).

Brontë, Charlotte. *Jane Eyre* (Penguin, 2006). [1847]

Bulgakov, Mikhail. *Master and Margarita*, trans. Michael Glenny (Vintage, 2010). [1940/1973]

Butterworth, Jez. *Jerusalem* (NHB, 2009).

Camus, Albert. *L'Étranger* (Gallimard, 1957). [1942]

Capote, Truman. *In Cold Blood* (Penguin, 2000). [1965]

Carter, Angela. *Nights at the Circus* (Vintage, 1994). [1984]

Cassirer, Ernst. *The Philosophy of Symbolic Forms*, 4 vols, trans. Ralph Manheim (Yale University Press, 1953–96).

Cervantes, Miguel de. *Don Quixote* (Penguin, 2003). [1605]

Derrida, Jacques. 'Plato's Pharmacy', in *Dissemination*, trans. Barbara Johnson (London: Athlone Press, 1981), pp. 61–171.

Dickens, Charles. *David Copperfield* (Wordsworth Classics, 1992). [1849–50]

——*Bleak House* (Penguin, 1996). [1852–3]

——*Little Dorrit* (Wordsworth Classics, 1992). [1855–7]

Dumas, Alexandre. *Le Comte de Monte-Cristo* (Pocket, 1995). [1844–5]

Eikhenbaum, Boris. 'Leskov i sovremennaia proza' ['Leskov and Contemporary Prose'] in Eikhenbaum, *Literatura: teoriia, kritika, polemika* (Priboi, 1927), pp. 210–25.

Engels, Friedrich. *Dialectics of Nature*, trans. Clemens Dutt (Lawrence and Wishart, 1940). [1883]

Freud, Sigmund. *Civilization and its Discontents* (Penguin, 2004). [1930]

Frye, Northrop. *Anatomy of Criticism: Four Essays* (Princeton University Press, 1957).

Goethe, Johann Wolfgang von. *Wilhelm Meister*, trans. H.M. Waidson (Alma Classics, 2013). [1795–6/1821]

Gogol, Nikolai. 'The Overcoat' [1842], in *The Diary of a Madman, The Government Inspector and other Stories*, trans. Ronald Wilks (Penguin, 2005), pp. 140–73.

Grass, Günter. *The Tin Drum* (Vintage, 2010). [1959]

Heliodorus of Emesa. *Aethiopica*, trans. Walter Lamb (Dent, 1997). [c. 220–250 A.D.]

Homer, *The Iliad*, trans. Alexander Pope (Penguin, 1996). [760–710 B.C.]

Hugo, Victor. *Les Misérables* (Garnier, 1963). [1862]

Jakobson, Roman. 'Noveishaia russkaia poeziia' ['Recent Russian Poetry'], in Jakobson, *Selected Writings*, vol. 5 (Mouton, 1979), pp. 299–354.

Keats, John. *The Complete Poems* (Penguin, 1988).

Kelman, James. *How Late it Was, How Late* (Secker & Warburg, 1994).

Lenin, Vladimir. *Materialism and Empirio-criticism* (Martin Lawrence, 1927). [1909]

Marcuse, Herbert. 'The Affirmative Character of Culture', in *Negations: Essays in Critical Theory* (Boston: Beacon Press, 1968), pp. 88–133.

Marx, Karl. 'Theses on Feuerbach', http://www.marxists.org/archive/marx/works/1845/theses/ [1845/1924]

Milton, John. *Paradise Lost* (Penguin, 2003). [1667]

Peace, David. *GB84* (Faber & Faber 2014). [2004]

Petronius. *Satyricon* (Oxford University Press, 1997). [c. 27–66 A.D.]

Pushkin, Alexander. *Eugene Onegin*, trans. Stanley Mitchell (Penguin, 2008). [1825–32]

Rabelais, François. *Gargantua and Pantagruel*, trans. M.A. Screech (Penguin, 2006). [c. 1532–64]

Rhys, Jean. *Wide Sargasso Sea* (Penguin, 2000). [1966]

Saussure, Ferdinand de. *Course in General Linguistics* (Fontana/Collins, 1974). [1916]

Scott, Walter. *Marmion* (Clarendon Press, 1889). [1808]

Stalin, Joseph. *Concerning Marxism in Linguistics* (Soviet News, 1950).

Turgenev, Ivan. 'Andrei Kolosov', trans. Constance Garnett, in *The Diary of a Superfluous Man: And Other Stories* (Tark, 2009), pp. 117–43. [1844]

Welsh, Irvine. *Trainspotting* (Minerva, 1994).

3. SELECTED CRITICAL WORKS ON BAKHTIN

Brandist, Craig. *The Bakhtin Circle: Philosophy, Culture, Politics* (Pluto Press, 2002).

Clark, Katerina and Michael Holquist. *Mikhail Bakhtin* (Harvard University Press, 1984).

Emerson, Caryl. *The First Hundred Years of Mikhail Bakhtin* (Princeton University Press, 1997).

Falconer, Rachel, Carol Adlam, Vitalii Makhlin and Alastair Renfrew (eds). *Face to Face: Bakhtin in Russia and the West* (Sheffield Academic Press, 1997).

Hirschkop, Ken. *Mikhail Bakhtin: An Aesthetic for Democracy* (Oxford University Press, 1999).

Hirschkop, Ken and David Shepherd (eds). *Bakhtin and Cultural Theory* (Manchester University Press, 1989). [2nd edn, 2001]

Mayerfeld Bell, Michael and Michael Gardiner (eds). *Bakhtin and the Human Sciences: No Last Words* (Sage, 1998).

Morson, Gary Saul and Caryl Emerson. *Mikhail Bakhtin: Creation of a Prosaics* (Stanford University Press, 1990).

Pechey, Graham. *Mikhail Bakhtin: The Word in the World* (Routledge, 2007).

Renfrew, Alastair. *Towards a New Material Aesthetics: Bakhtin, Genre and the Fates of Literary Theory* (Legenda, 2006).

Tihanov, Galin. *The Master and the Slave: Lukács, Bakhtin, and the Ideas of their Time* (Oxford University Press, 2000).

Todorov, Tzvetan. *Mikhail Bakhtin: The Dialogical Principle*, trans. Wlad Godzich (University of Minnesota Press, 1984).

INDEX

consciousness 72–3; and
dialogism 80, 83, 89, 91–2; and
heteroglossia 99–100, 103, 110,
111; the literary work as 124,
146–8, 163; and speech genres
152–4, 156, 166

Vinogradov, Viktor 60
Voloshinov, Valentin 5, 8, 12–14,
18, 20–21, 58, 60, 82, 91, 98,
147, 148, 152, 156, 169;
'Discourse in Life and Discourse
in Poetry' 61, 63–8, 75, 102, 152;
Freudianism 9, 13, 34–6;

*Marxism and the Philosophy of
Language* 9, 14, 61–74, 80–1,
143, 152, 170
voice 76–8, 81–3, 85–6, 101, 104–8,
160, 165
Vossler, Karl 62

Welsh, Irvine 107, 151
Wittgenstein, Ludwig 58
Wordsworth, William 48–9

Zephaniah, Benjamin 109
Zhirmunskii, Viktor 60
Zvezda [The Star] 13

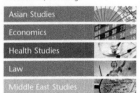